The Play of Your Life

Your Program for
Finding the **Career
of Your Dreams—**
And a Step-by-Step
Guide to
Making It a Reality

Colleen A. Sabatino

RODALE

Library of Congress Cataloging-in-Publication Data

Sabatino, Colleen A.
    The play of your life : your program for finding the career of your dreams—and a step-by-step guide to making it a reality / Colleen A. Sabatino.
        p.   cm.
    Includes index.
    ISBN 1–57954–964–0 paperback
    1. Vocational guidance.   2. Career development.   I. Title.
HF5381.S224   2004
650.14—dc22   2004006783

Distributed to the trade by Holtzbrinck Publishers

2   4   6   8   10   9   7   5   3   1   paperback

WE **INSPIRE** AND **ENABLE** PEOPLE TO IMPROVE
THEIR LIVES AND THE WORLD AROUND THEM

FOR MORE OF OUR PRODUCTS
WWW.RODALESTORE.COM
(800) 848-4735

To my mother, Susan Sandberg,

for her inspiration and gift of communication

CONTENTS

FOREWORD

When I first met Colleen Sabatino, more than 5 years ago, I was immediately impressed with her energy, enthusiasm, and commitment to the career development process. From an early age, she has dedicated her life, education, and career to understanding and, ultimately, greatly enhancing the career development process. Seldom do you encounter an individual with such passion, generosity, and a willingness to share her time, expertise, and unbridled enthusiasm.

In *The Play of Your Life,* Colleen has given both new and experienced career seekers a great gift. You now have a resource to develop a comprehensive approach to managing your career. The book starts with a framework for interpreting how values, temperament, personality, and interests impact career choice. This evaluation process leads to a useful guide for creating résumés and cover letters, as well as preparing for interviews. And finally, to ensure a workable strategy, the book offers a set of practical approaches to managing a productive and strategic career search. It is an easy read—full of useful content applicable to even the most difficult cases in career development.

For many career seekers, suggestions and information from well-meaning family members and friends can create confusion and anxiety, even before their career search starts. In this book, Colleen emphasizes the importance of following a structured process for navigating your career path, to help you secure the career that is right for you.

As a result, she is able to clearly connect the stages of career development:

- Career exploration—obtaining clarity and direction
- Campaign development—clearly communicating career goals and objectives
- Career search implementation—developing action plans for realizing your goals

Colleen encourages you to find yourself at center stage. She gives useful suggestions for identifying what is important to you in your career, how to articulate your value to prospective employers and ways to implement a career search that is organized and appropriate to achieving your end goal—a satisfying career.

One of the most common questions asked of me by clients is "What books do you recommend for guidance?" My dilemma has always been with the choice of a resource that presents practical, simple, and yet individualized advice that encompasses all areas of the career development continuum. This book has solved this dilemma.

Colleen teaches you how to be true to your unique self and use this self-awareness to seek a career that feels more like play than work. I predict that for all career seekers, *The Play of Your Life* will become a dog-eared, well-loved resource. Enjoy!

Joyce Domijan
President
ACDI, Columbus, Ohio

ACKNOWLEDGMENTS

I want to thank Joyce Domijan for bringing her insights and writing expertise to this wonderful project, and for making my voice heard throughout the book. I knew from the moment she became the president of the ACDI office in Columbus, Ohio, that she totally understood my philosophy about career development. I am grateful for her friendship and hard work.

Thank you, Paula Chandler, for helping to interpret the work I do and for offering your wisdom and talents as a career management professional. As an ACDI partner, you make our company stronger and even more valuable to clients.

Thank you, Leah Chandler, for fine-tuning the book and for your great outreach efforts to the many colleges and universities that use our model in supporting their students and graduates.

I owe a debt of gratitude to my family and friends who supported me through the writing of this book. I appreciate beyond words all my clients who have shared their personal and professional growth and development and offered their personal stories and experiences so that others could benefit from this book. A special thanks to Christa Juenger, Stacey Stormer, Anthony Bosca, Rosemarie Sabatino, Leighann Davis, Edward Sabatino, Bob Maloney, and Estelle Winsett for reviewing the book during its creation.

Finally, I am grateful to the people who have helped me negotiate the new terrain of the publishing world: Elizabeth Kaplan, Scott Waxman, Jeremy Katz, and Luke Weinstock.

INTRODUCTION

The Play of Your Life is based on the premise that the world is your stage and you are the star of your own life. I chose to make the metaphor of the play central to this book because it best highlights the core principles and lessons I have gleaned in my 10 years of experience in the field of career counseling. It also provides a useful framework that enables me to construct an indi-

> *"If you do what you like, you never really work. Your work is your play."*
> —*Hans Selye*

vidual program for each reader, whether starting out in a first career or making a successful career transition. I hope this book raises the curtain on a new stage in your life—one that creates the possibility of making career choices that turn every day of your life into a meaningful and rewarding new act.

The action of the play and, by extension, your life can only truly begin once the leading character is fully defined on stage. Thus, the object of the first half of the book is to help you find yourself center stage. After that, the program guides you through the practical steps necessary to implement an effective action plan that will turn your work into your play. Throughout this book, I have demonstrated the application of the processes outlined in each chapter through examples of my clients' experiences in career counseling.

People too often think of "playing a role" as something artificial, at odds with reality. But in actuality, everyone plays a series of roles. People become by pretending; we play as children before we get a chance as adults. Our process of growth is in large part a willingness to take new risks, to take new roles.

The more "roles" we play and the more we have tried, the more we become a unique and united self. The simple person is less than a person. The complex person is an army on the move.

As participants in the play of your life, you are invited into the process of defining yourself. You are encouraged to move out, anywhere, into the world, trying on different lives for size and feeling the fit or discomfort. In the play of your life, the stage is uncontaminated by the fears that halt much of your ability to take risks and grow. By allowing yourself to role-play your perfect self, you will gain strength and confidence. In this process, you will build the armor to overcome or at least understand your fears and equip yourself to acquire a greater sense of satisfaction.

ACT ONE

Career Exploration—
Finding Yourself
Center Stage

The Stage

PLAYS ARE MORE than a form of entertainment. They are artistic media in which feelings are expressed about subjects that have meaning and value. A play conveys a deeper message woven throughout the plot that enriches lives and promotes reflection and growth. As you develop the

> *"All the world's a stage, and each of us its actors."*
> —William Shakespeare

play of your life, it is critical to understand what gives meaning to your life and what you value most.

This chapter begins with identifying your values because career satisfaction is highly dependent on how well your work environment reflects your values. According to statistics, 8 out of 10 people leave their careers, whether by choice or not, because of a misalignment between their own values and the values of the organization for which they work. An awareness of your personal values is critical to finding satisfying work.

In turn, your values will create the foundation for casting your leading role and developing your plot. The values assessment will help establish what is meaningful to you. It will define the environment you need to perform at your very best. Also, you will identify the leadership style that best fits your values so you can select an organizational culture that is in alignment with those values.

Values

While what you value plays a critical role in choosing a career path, you may not have thought recently about what you really value in life. When was the last time someone asked you what you most value in life? When was the last time you explored this territory, to understand the deepest parts of yourself? If you are like most people, it is not something you do on a regular basis. And yet assessing values is imperative to career exploration. Since the most common reason for career dissatisfaction is a conflict between personal values and values that are highly regarded in a particular work environment, finding a great "value fit" is essential if you are going to be satisfied with your work.

By establishing a clear understanding of your values, you will be able to assess whether a particular organization or environment is right for you. By understanding how your values affect your choice of leadership style and work environment, you will know why you like or dislike certain styles or environments. You can then be proactive in selecting your appropriate leadership and work environment.

The first step toward understanding your values is to complete an assessment that helps depict your personal value type. From this assessment, you will obtain a clear picture of what drives your career decisions. The next step is to examine how your personal values impact your preferences for various leadership styles, environments, and types of careers. You can then select careers that will fulfill your deepest needs because they will align with your core values.

Prioritize Your Values

The following values assessment is a learning instrument that provides a basis for identifying your unique values. By knowing what is most important to you, you will be able to more clearly articulate what you want out of your career. This assessment helps you prioritize the values that are most important to you.

VALUES ASSESSMENT

Instructions: For each of the following groups of three words, place a 3 by the word that is *most* important to you and a 1 by the word that is *least* important. Place a 2 next to the remaining word in the group.

1. a. Power   _____
   b. Style   _____
   c. People   _____

2. a. Thinking   _____
   b. Practicality _____
   c. Winning   _____

3. a. Taste   _____
   b. Unselfishness _____
   c. Reason   _____

4. a. Tangibility   _____
   b. Overcoming _____
   c. Appearance _____

5. a. Helping   _____
   b. Science   _____
   c. Efficiency   _____

6. a. Control   _____
   b. Charm   _____
   c. Kindness   _____

7. a. Knowledge _____
   b. Utility   _____
   c. Position   _____

8. a. Culture   _____
   b. Warmth   _____
   c. Analysis   _____

9. a. Usefulness _____
    b. Command _____
    c. Refinement _____

10. a. Aid _____
    b. Information _____
    c. Application _____

11. a. Conquest _____
    b. Art _____
    c. Sympathy _____

12. a. Learning _____
    b. Production _____
    c. Strength _____

13. a. Harmony _____
    b. Giving _____
    c. Solutions _____

14. a. Prosperity _____
    b. Struggles _____
    c. Form _____

15. a. Understanding _____
    b. Logic _____
    c. Wealth _____

16. a. Influence _____
    b. Elegance _____
    c. Charity _____

17. a. Explanation _____
    b. Profit _____
    c. Authority _____

18. a. Symmetry _____
    b. Freedom _____
    c. Theories _____

19. a. Effectiveness _____
    b. Privilege _____
    c. Beauty _____

20. a. Assistance _____
    b. Research _____
    c. Earnings _____

Values Assessment Scoring Sheet

Instructions: Enter your scores from the values assessment form in the spaces on the opposite page. Add the scores in each column and enter the total for the column in the space provided. The highest score indicates your value type and is ranked number one. The remaining four columns can then be ranked based on their descending numeric scores.

Driver	Creator	Humanitarian	Pursuer	Maximizer
Ia _____	Ib _____	Ic _____	2a _____	2b _____
6a _____	6b _____	6c _____	7a _____	7b _____
IIa _____	IIb _____	IIc _____	I2a _____	I2b _____
I6a _____	I6b _____	I6c _____	I7a _____	I7b _____
2c _____	3a _____	3b _____	3c _____	4a _____
7c _____	8a _____	8b _____	8c _____	9a _____
I2c _____	I3a _____	I3b _____	I3c _____	I4a _____
I7c _____	I8a _____	I8b _____	I8c _____	I9a _____
4b _____	4c _____	5a _____	5b _____	5c _____
9b _____	9c _____	I0a _____	I0b _____	I0c _____
I4b _____	I4c _____	I5a _____	I5b _____	I5c _____
I9b _____	I9c _____	20a _____	20b _____	20c _____
Total _____	Total _____	Total _____	Total _____	Total _____
Rank _____	Rank _____	Rank _____	Rank _____	Rank _____

Determine Your Values

Below are descriptions of the five value types. In conjunction with the results of the values assessment, these descriptions will help you discover where you best fit. As you read the descriptions of the value types, imagine the characteristics and environments that each value type creates. Accompanying client stories show how others used their values assessments to clarify what was important to them. As you read the descriptions and vignettes, try to envision what leadership style, work environment, and career insights emerge as a result of your value type. The values assessment gives you a starting place by identifying your predominant value type. Does this value type seem to fit you well?

THE DRIVER

- If your value type is The Driver, you are motivated by an environment that encourages advancement and upward mobility.

- This value type allows you to influence others with your vision while providing you with status symbols like a large office with a window or a company car and an expense account.

- The Driver measures success in dollars, so salary is very important to you; however, your ultimate goal is obtaining a position of authority within an organization.

Mike is a client who represents The Driver value type well. Mike completed his degree in economics and business administration from a top-tier university and started his career in a management-training program for a large bank in Nashville, Tennessee. Mike liked using on-campus interviews to secure a position in a stable industry. This particular bank saw college recruiting as a vehicle for identifying talent and molding its new hires to fit the company's internal career-advancement track. Mike also liked the rotations of a management-training program because he was able to assess what path would most quickly lead to promotion and more money. He selected the fast track and began climbing the corporate ladder.

Mike thrived in this environment. He enjoyed the company car, increasingly larger office space and expense account, and the ability to move up by following clearly defined expectations. Mike also liked securing titles that had "vice president" on the business card. These aspects of his career were great. After 5 years, Mike was recruited by a customer whose company developed specialty products for the banking industry. Mike loved the attention and the increase in compensation. The move was a good one, and he went on to head up the research and development team for new products.

Several years later, another recruiter called him to join a start-up that was competing in a similar market, and Mike went for it. But once at the company, Mike ran into a political struggle with several key people; Mike lost. When he started his career-counseling program, he had just been asked to leave the company and was completely shocked.

During his career exploration process, Mike decided that he was ready to take his drive for power and success to the next level and start his own company. His approach, and appropriately so, has been to identify profitable companies in growth markets and seek out opportunities to purchase an existing operation or possibly buy a franchise within that market. Mike is about business and winning. Therefore, the business he chooses to acquire is not determined by passion for a certain product or service or his visionary thinking. His passion is fueled by his desire for power and authority.

THE CREATOR

- If your value type is The Creator, you are motivated by an environment that possesses beauty, symmetry, and harmony.

- This value type is dedicated to the artistic episodes of life. Style and charm describe this value type.

- An optimum environment for The Creator allows you to be self-sufficient and individualistic.

- Good taste, style, and elegant surroundings are what drive your interest in making money.

- Status is also important. You do not associate with just anyone or belong to just any organization. This value type appreciates the "good" organizations, has the "best" clients, and travels first-class.

Anthony is The Creator value type. He studied creative writing at a small liberal arts college in the Northwest and grew up attending gallery openings sponsored by his family. He went on to become an avid art collector himself.

He plays guitar as a hobby and pursues his passion for photography through frequent photo shoots and weekends away to explore nature and capture its beauty on film. Anthony also enjoys cooking and appreciates fine wines and good cuisine.

His career started in marketing for a high-end manufacturer of fine leather goods. He traveled extensively throughout the world on behalf of the company and developed relationships with some of the best advertising agencies to ensure that his company's products were prominently featured in magazines and fashion shows. Anthony truly enjoyed his career, but the company ran into financial difficulties and he was forced to explore opportunities outside the company.

At first he welcomed the change and felt some relief after months of building pressure within the company. Anthony had obtained his most recent position through a family connection, so he had never really stopped to explore his own career path. After several months of weighing the pros and cons of trying to turn one of his hobbies into a full-fledged career, he began to recognize that his current lifestyle required more than what he would make as an art collector, photographer, novelist, musician, or chef. Knowing his creative talents are far superior to most, he set out to develop the most impressive portfolio he could create and identified the most respected advertising agencies in town.

Anthony hand-delivered a beautifully packaged professional biography and samples of his work and requested face-to-face meetings. Of the dozen or so firms he visited, nearly half agreed to a meeting. Within a few short months, Anthony landed a position with a small but very successful advertising agency about three blocks from his home. His intention was to enjoy his family a little more than he had been able to before and help grow the company to a sizable firm. His long-term objective was to buy the agency from the current owner, who had expressed this interest early in their relationship.

After several years, however, Anthony began to feel like he was stagnating. The agency was not growing, and the current owner was not giving up his creative or business authority as quickly as Anthony would have liked. During the course of his self-analysis, Anthony recognized his need to exercise creative liberty and control of his future. Working for another creative type, while possible, was not ideal. He wanted to own his own company but also knew that he had to be excited by the product. It would have to be a product that was the best of its class and catered to an audience that appreciates the finer things in life.

Anthony began analyzing companies on the market. He looked into furniture stores, a sports equipment company, and a printing business, and then came upon an eyeglass store that sold very attractive frames to people who appreciated eyewear as fashion more than necessity. He conducted due diligence on all of the prospects, but it was clear when he described the different options that the eyeglass company was most appealing. Anthony went on to buy the company and now owns and operates a chain of the stores. Anthony's career choices are driven by his need to be creative and appreciate the more refined episodes of life.

THE HUMANITARIAN

- If your value type is The Humanitarian, you are motivated by an environment that improves the lives of others, allowing you to be kind, sympathetic, warm, and giving.

- This value type appreciates charity, unselfishness, and the freedom of others and is apt to offer aid and assistance to others, as well as understanding.

- The Humanitarian value type contributes to another's well-being. Acting for materialistic gain without first considering the consequences on other people is against your nature.

Ron is a client who represents The Humanitarian value type. He is currently an outplacement consultant who serves as an onsite career counselor for a large corporate client who is in the process of downsizing thousands of workers across the country. Ron sought career counseling for himself because he felt disenchanted by the quality of services being extended to the employees and similarly frustrated by the lack of interest expressed by the employees in the programs offered to them.

Ron began his career as a mental health counselor for a large state-funded agency. In this nonprofit organization, he administered care to all types of people troubled by various mental issues. After 15 years, he began to burn out and left the agency to join an Employee Assistance Program (EAP) organization that provided counseling services to employees of large corporations. After 7 years, he became discouraged with the tight restrictions imposed upon them by insurance companies. He would just be getting somewhere with his clients, and they would run out of sessions. His role of surface medical care and referral left him feeling unfulfilled.

Ron decided that his background in counseling disgruntled employees would lend itself well to the outplacement industry, and he applied for a consulting job with one of the three largest outplacement firms in the country. Ron believed that employees would be very interested in receiving his services but found that many employees saw the group workshops as belittling and inefficient after giving a life of service to the company. Instead of feeling helpful, Ron began to wonder if his role was more harmful than beneficial.

Ron loved career counseling, but he needed to provide a quality of service that was not determined by an insurance company policy or employer trying to cut costs at every corner. He needed to counsel people who sought guidance and support rather than those mandated to attend a job search seminar. Upon review of his values, he knew he was in the right profession but was exercising his talents in the wrong industry. Ron subsequently opened his own private practice offering career counseling directly to individuals. While the financial reward is less predictable than at the large outplacement firm, he feels in complete alignment with his core needs, and it has made all the difference.

THE PURSUER

- If your value type is The Pursuer, you are motivated by an environment that values truth and knowledge above all else. Thinking, learning, reasoning, probing, analyzing, and explaining are important to you.

- An environment for The Pursuer allows you to be critical, logical, and empirical. It values science, research, information, and theory.

- For this value type, not only knowledge but the organization and cataloging of knowledge are important. This allows you to solve problems, develop theories, and form questions.

Laura is a client who represents The Pursuer value type. Laura is an attorney for a large, prestigious firm in Minneapolis. She was a top pick by the firm upon her graduation from law school and has been groomed for partner since the beginning. A bright and highly disciplined person, Laura excelled in the firm and took on increasingly demanding clients and higher-profile projects.

As Laura continued to bring more value to the firm, her compensation grew, and she felt gratified and content. Then her role began to change as she rose through the ranks. Laura was asked to supervise attorneys within her division, and partners began inviting her on business development calls. While flattered by the attention and the authority to lead the department, her satisfaction began to decline. Laura did not enjoy managing people, and she did not like sales. It was at this time that she was passed over for partner. Laura knew that sales and management were expectations of partners, but she had not anticipated herself in these roles, even though she was on the track to partner.

Upon analysis of her value type, Laura recognized that her career selection to practice law was a good fit. She was not going to be happy, though, as a partner and was feeling pressure to leave the firm. Laura began talking with several close friends about her predicament and explained that she enjoyed her expertise in the profession and simply wanted to be compensated and relied on to offer fantastic counsel. She did not need to become a partner in a large firm. After Laura made her interests clear, a friend suggested she pursue a position as general counsel to a local corporation that needed in-house legal support. Laura began to network confidentially with a few trustworthy contacts and within 4 months made the switch to the corporate world. Laura's value type helped her to recognize where the misalignment was coming from in her career and make decisions based on that knowledge.

THE MAXIMIZER

- If your value type is The Maximizer, you are motivated by an environment that is practical and useful. You focus on pragmatic achievement and the production of something tangible and useful.

- For this value type, efficiency and effectiveness are measured by profit and prosperity. You may judge the value of others by their wealth or income as well as their ability to produce.

- The Maximizer is dedicated to getting the business advancing upwardly as soon and as easily as possible. In pursuing goals or achievements, this value type tends to take risks in order to minimize input.

Jeff represents this value type. He started his career as a sales associate for a large telecommunications company and enjoyed 6 years as a top performer in his territory. His boss was hands-off as long as he met his quota, and allowed Jeff to work whatever hours suited him best. Jeff found numerous ways to cut corners and still get the job done and prided himself on identifying shortcuts that made his job much easier than the other sales representatives'.

He treated everyone, especially the team who assisted him once a new customer was signed up, with great respect and appreciation. Jeff did not particularly enjoy maintaining ongoing relationships with his customers except for surface encounters: face time and social visits. Knowing this, he always gave his support staff special gifts and treats to thank them for taking over where he would, sometimes prematurely, leave them off. This system worked well until Jeff got reassigned to a new territory with a different boss. Under the new leadership, Jeff's quick pace and crafty approach were not acceptable. Everything was by the book, and no shortcuts or support from others was tolerated. He quickly became unhappy.

When Jeff started his career-counseling program, he explained that his career path was not driven by what he sold but how he sold. He needed an environment that gave him the freedom to meet the sales quota without a lot of hand-holding or micromanagement. He chose sales for the freedom and liked being compensated for his performance, not how many hours he clocked or how well he followed standard operating procedures. Jeff had also become accustomed to a lucrative lifestyle and could not imagine a career move that did not offer a high income potential.

Since Jeff was so personable, he realized that he knew the vast majority of professionals in his industry. After a thorough review of his values and strengths, Jeff decided that as a recruiter he could achieve his financial goals and still retain the freedom of doing his own thing. Jeff left the telecommunications industry as a salesperson and came back the next day as a recruiter specializing in the telecommunications industry. He used his vast network and contacts at all levels of organizations to help him obtain hard-to-get information for his clients. He worked his own hours, and while the hours were sometimes long, they were used in his way and he was compensated handsomely for the results he produced.

Your Value Type

Pick the one value type that strikes you as the truest all-around fit for you. This is your primary value type in the play of your life. Since most people do not fit neatly into one type, you may then add those key elements from the other descriptions until you have captured what feels like a complete description that fully represents you.

A combination of several value types may reflect your core values more accurately. Some combinations of values appear to be mutually supportive, while others appear to conflict to varying degrees.

Select the two highest-ranked values from your values assessment and read the description of this combination. See if this combination describes your values accurately.

Driver and Creator: You want to be in an organization that serves a grand purpose. You appreciate leadership that allows you to exercise your individuality and express your beliefs freely.

Driver and Humanitarian: You want a position of power in an organization dedicated to improving the lives of others. Your leadership style is paternalistic to others, and you appreciate leaders who treat staff as family.

Driver and Pursuer: You want to be in an intellectual environment. You appreciate environments that allow you to use your knowledge, which in turn leads to recognition, influence, and control.

Driver and Maximizer: You desire an environment reflective of the successful American business. You are well-suited for an executive position. This serves your goal for economic success, power, and position.

Creator and Humanitarian: You instinctively gravitate toward environments that focus on human needs. You appreciate opportunities that allow you to express emotion and concern for others.

Creator and Pursuer: You want an organization that combines a sound basis of logic and explanations with opportunities to express your feelings and sensitivities to beauty.

Creator and Maximizer: You want an organization that allows you to be practical and efficient while pursuing style and beauty.

When Ken became a client, he looked exhausted and totally drained. He had a 10-year, fabulously successful career for a large corporation. He spent his first 5 years as a marketing manager, then transitioned to an account executive. While his income had increased by leaps and bounds in the past 5 years, his satisfaction with his career was waning. He constantly felt completely depleted of energy at the end of the day, and this was having a very negative impact on his "family time." Ken wanted to explore his options to see if he could find a career that would be less draining on a daily basis. While going through the process of assessing his value type, there were two factors that really stood out for Ken. First, he was a Maximizer, preferring to see tangible results for his efforts. This was somewhat at odds with the daily routine of an account executive, which requires developing long-term relationships involving lengthy sales cycles. Second, his primary value was that of a Creator, and he loved working when he had the chance to be creative, imaginative, and innovative. In reviewing his career history in combination with his new knowledge, he realized that he was happiest and most satisfied when he was working in marketing. Ken subsequently applied for a marketing vice president position with his company and was able to combine his knowledge of the sales process with his passion for the more creative side of the business.

Humanitarian and Pursuer: You seek an organization that serves others through knowledge. You need leaders who appreciate your desire to help others to become more rational.

Humanitarian and Maximizer: You want an organization in which goals for productivity and satisfaction are equally important. You want leaders who allow you to encourage economic opportunity because it benefits people.

Pursuer and Maximizer: You want to be in an organization that uses practical applications of knowledge. You need leaders who allow you to be inventive and pragmatic in your approach to science.

After reading the value-type combinations, list the combined value type that best reflects your values:

_____

_____

_____

Values and Your Career

Now that you have a clearer understanding of your values, you can use this information to clarify why certain leaders and work environments are preferable to you. Take a moment to reflect on the leadership and work environments you have experienced in the past. Now think about the leadership and work environment that will provide you the greatest satisfaction in the future. The following exercises are designed to help you clarify what type of leadership and work environment best suit your personal values.

Leadership

Values as they relate to leadership can best be understood by examining how leadership has interacted within organization in your past experiences. Review the following leadership indicators and check those that you have personally experienced.

Experiences with Leadership

_____ Acknowledged when I did well

_____ Gave me performance evaluations to let me know where I stood

_____ Gave me lots of freedom

_____ Gave me recognition and praise in front of others

_____ Allowed me to participate in the planning and decision making that affected me

_____ Allowed me to attend staff meetings

_____ Looked over my shoulder

_____ Stepped in often

_____ Established procedures

_____ Checked my work often

_____ Required infrequent reports from me

_____ Was rarely present

_____ Was receptive to my ideas

_____ Had a hands-off management style

_____ Served as a mentor

What value types were present in your past work environments and in the leadership of the organization? What did you like and dislike? What indicators were most meaningful to you and would you want to see in your next career?

_____

_____

_____

_____

_____

Descriptions of Leaders

To continue deepening your exploration of leadership styles that fit your values, read each quality below and circle the five that are most important to you in a leader.

Innovative	Pleasant	Mentally challenging
Energetic	Good listener	Natural
Loyal	Practical	Intelligent
Helpful	Organized	Ambitious
Respectful	Athletic	Professional
Even-tempered	Selfless	Technically competent
Friendly	Family-oriented	Assertive
Honest	Well-informed	Nonjudgmental
Creative	Courteous	Extroverted
Artistic	Receptive	Introverted
Diligent	Humorous	

Now it is time to synthesize the information you have gathered. Using the results of the values assessment, your past experiences with leadership, and the qualities of leaders, answer the following questions:

1. What is the management style(s) of the leader you most respect and want to emulate?

_____

_____

2. What is the communication style(s) of the leader you respect and want to emulate?

_____

_____

Work Environment

The elements you value in a work environment can be understood by remembering what was desirable for you in the past. Review the descriptions of work environments and select those that you have personally experienced.

Experiences with Work Environments

_____ Colleagues respected me as a person

_____ Attractive environment, physically appealing

_____ Got along well with my coworkers

_____ Informed of what was going on in my company

_____ Felt I was responsible for something significant

_____ Driven by clearly defined policies and procedures

_____ Limited change

_____ Established chain of command

_____ Allowed some input

_____ Responsive to employee input

_____ Encouraged teamwork

_____ Valued new ideas

_____ Reacted quickly to market changes

_____ Few established policies

_____ Fair company policies

Which aspects of the work environment are most important to you in your next career?

_____

_____

_____

_____

_____

_____

Descriptions of Work Environments

In order to deepen your understanding of what you want in a work environment, review each pair of words describing an aspect of the work environment and circle the word in each pair that is most important to you.

Business casual   vs.   Suit

Changing   vs.   Stable

High risk   vs.   Low risk

Commission-based	vs.	Salary-based
Informal	vs.	Formal
Unstructured	vs.	Structured
Individual reward	vs.	Team reward
Flat	vs.	Hierarchical
Caregiving	vs.	Caretaking

Now let's pull it all together. Reflecting back on what you learned about your value type and prior experiences with leadership and work environments, answer the following questions to help clarify what is most important to you when choosing a career.

1. What is the environment you most appreciate and want to be in?

_____

_____

_____

2. What is the culture you most respect and want to work in?

_____

_____

_____

Brenda is a great example of the importance of a "value match" in your career. She was a manager and editor in the publishing industry and was working for a large corporation. The size and the culture of the organization contributed to a high-pressure, fast-paced, impersonal work environment. The leadership of the corporation practiced top-down management—assigning middle managers projects for completion and allowing very little input or creativity. Due to the size of the organization, there were lots of rules and regulations to enforce, and little leeway was given to address individual problems and concerns.

Brenda was suffocating in this environment and believed that it was time to change careers. While she had been happy and satisfied in the past with editing and publishing, she now felt burnt-out and discouraged. It had come to the point that when the alarm rang in the morning, she dreaded the thought of getting up and going to work. In reviewing the results of Brenda's values assessment, it was clear that several characteristics of the leadership and work environment were at odds with her value type. She had a very strong Humanitarian value type. At her very core, she was motivated by her need to improve the lives of others. The large, impersonal corporate environment was not allowing her to do that.

In the end, Brenda didn't need to change careers to find happiness and fulfillment. She simply needed to change her environment. She accepted a position with a small publishing firm. In her first weeks, she excitedly called to describe the "family culture" of the smaller environment. She talked about collaboration and the team mentality and how everyone pitched in to help. Her smile resonated right through the phone line—she had found a home and a great values match.

In the play of your life, values are at the core of excellent decision making. Knowing what you value in life and how to relate your values to career choices gives you the ability to select a career that is so satisfying that it will not feel like work. Instead, it will feel like play. A great plot and good acting can make for a decent play, but if it leaves you unfulfilled, it will not be an event you would wish to experience again.

The process of finding yourself center stage starts with your values, but equally important are the characteristics and traits that stem from your personality preferences. Well, Finding Yourself Center Stage is the title of the first act. The next chapter uses additional assessments and exercises to deepen your analysis and more fully explain the innate qualities that emerge within you. Becoming clear on these aspects of yourself will provide great insights for learning about your strengths, motivations, and natural gifts. The next chapter is called The Leading Role because it is dedicated to bringing forth those important pieces of you that determine the role you gravitate to most instinctively, the environments you are drawn to, and qualities you naturally exhibit in your career. With a clear understanding of your values—the foundation from which you build your career—you are now ready to cast your leading role.

The Leading Role

YOU HAVE SEEN how an assessment of your values leads to a better understanding of what kind of work environment will be most conducive to success in your career. Now you will examine your overall orientation to life to better understand the kinds of qualities you should be exhibiting in your career. The following exercises and assessments help iden-

> *"To be or not to be: that is the question."*
>
> —*William Shakespeare*

tify the conditions in which you are most comfortable and the kind of work you gravitate to most naturally. Your values help explain what kind of environment is best suited to you, but it is your overall orientation to life and personality preferences that clarify what kind of work you are naturally fit to pursue. The role you cast for yourself in the play of your life is best understood by analyzing these innate preferences that shape what you like to do.

First, it is important to understand what personality preferences are. The following exercise will help illustrate what they are.

Sign your name on the line below:

_____

Sign your name, but this time use your *opposite* hand:

_____

Describe the experience of writing your name with the preferred hand. What about the nonpreferred hand?

Some people say . . .

Preferred hand: Feels natural, didn't think about it, effortless, looks neat, easy, comfortable

Nonpreferred hand: Feels unnatural, had to think, concentrate, required energy, awkward, clumsy

It is likely that you did not make a conscious choice to be left-handed or right-handed. A preference for one hand simply emerged. You still use both hands, but one is more comfortable, particularly for certain tasks like writing. The same holds true for personality preferences.

Just as you use both hands, you use personality preferences as well. All preferences are equally valuable, but some preferences are more natural and therefore are used more regularly, which helps them to develop into strengths.

One way to learn about your innate preferences is to take an assessment that helps describe behaviors to which you naturally gravitate. By knowing your personality preferences, you can more clearly identify career choices that lend themselves to your preferences. When you use your natural preferences to work, it is easier and more fun. It does not feel like work. It feels more like play. The objective of this chapter is to identify work activities that are a natural fit for you. This way you have a better chance of finding work that matches your preferences rather than simply picking a profession randomly.

To start, complete the following assessment to determine your preferences. Use the results of this preferences assessment to find the soliloquy that most resembles your unique leading role. Read all the solo parts and determine what leading role you cast yourself in for the play of your life. Since most people do not fit neatly into just one role, start with the one that is the best fit and then add those elements from other roles that represent you so that you have a complete and full description of your preferences and innate qualities.

PREFERENCES ASSESSMENT

Complete the assessment by circling the letter that describes your response. The statements are not meant to be taken literally but figuratively. After you read each statement, think about your personality preference and select the answer that best represents your natural approach to interacting with others, making decisions, perceiving the environment around you, or getting energized. There may be some statements where you agree with both responses. When this happens, try to select the response that is closer to your gut reaction. You may have learned to act or think a certain way over time because it serves you well, but for the purposes of this assessment, try to answer the questions by marking the response that elicits an immediate reaction.

1. During intermission, do you
    a. Interact with the people around you, even strangers
    b. Interact with your friends or not at all

2. Do you prefer plays that are more
    a. Realistic stories that apply to your life
    b. Based on universal ideas that make you think about the world differently

3. Are you more likely to

    a. Want to attend a performance

    b. Want to participate in a performance

4. When reviewing a play that was neither extraordinarily good nor bad, are you

    a. More critical

    b. More complimentary

5. When deciding on what play to see, do you go by

    a. Reviews and ratings it has received by notable sources

    b. Seeing if your friends or coworkers have seen it and general intuition

6. When you buy season tickets, do you

    a. Put all the dates on your calendar to ensure you can go

    b. Sometimes have to give tickets to friends because you've scheduled a trip

7. Do you

    a. Look at the season of plays, choose the ones you want to see, and order tickets

    b. Decide on Wednesday that you want to go to a play on Friday and see what tickets you can get

8. At the ticket counter, do you

    a. Chat with others even if you don't know them

    b. Stick to business and quietly wait your turn

9. Is it worse to

    a. Have unrealistic dreams of becoming a movie star

    b. Have only dreams that are attainable

10. Do you tend to prefer plays that have

    a. A plot that is easy to follow and a clear conclusion

    b. An existential theme that leaves the conclusion to the audience

11. Do you prefer plays that are

    a. About relationships and harmony

    b. Consistent and thought provoking

12. Would you identify more easily with a character that is more

    a. Logical

    b. Emotional

13. If you are meeting friends after the play, do you

    a. Have an exact meeting place

    b. Feel comfortable knowing that you will find each other eventually

14. When you make plans for dinner before a play, do you

    a. Determine the restaurant well in advance

    b. Call on the way and decide where you want to go

15. When the play ends, do you

    a. Stand immediately, clap, and maybe whistle

    b. Clap politely in your seat

16. Do you like plays that

    a. Say what they mean

    b. Use symbolism and metaphors to describe a point

17. When you watch a documentary, do you pay more attention to the

    a. Actual events and specific details

    b. Principles being illustrated

18. When you are enjoying a play, are you more involved through

    a. Your thoughts

    b. Your feelings

19. When watching an emotional play, are you
    a. More likely to show emotion
    b. Hold the emotional reaction inside

20. Does improvisation
    a. Make you nervous
    b. Excite you

21. When a play has an ambiguous ending, do you
    a. Feel annoyed with the author of the play
    b. Feel stimulated to speculate about all the possible endings

22. Does interacting with the audience
    a. Make you feel energized
    b. Make you wish intermission were over

23. Would you prefer playing a
    a. More practical role
    b. More fanciful role

24. Are you inclined to react to a play
    a. More literally, tracing the facts of the action
    b. More figuratively, expanding the ideas

25. When watching a play, do you find yourself
    a. Feeling the emotions of the characters
    b. Following the plot and anticipating what is next

26. Are you drawn to plays that are more
    a. Uplifting, with positive images of life
    b. Clearly constructed, with a thoughtful action and plot

27. When choosing a play, do you prefer to
    a. Make up your mind quickly
    b. Pick and choose at some length

28. Are you more satisfied by plays that
    a. Have a tight finish
    b. Leave the audience wanting more, speculative

29. Are you more likely to
    a. Go to a play alone
    b. Go with someone else

30. Are you more likely to pay attention to
    a. The stage design, costumes, and details of the stage
    b. The overall theme of the play

31. Do you prefer plays that are
    a. Action and adventure
    b. Fantasy and heroism

32. Do you want to see productions that give you
    a. A sense of the possibility in life
    b. A realistic, gritty image of the way things are

33. Do you prefer going to
    a. A musical production
    b. A drama

34. Do you prefer plays that are
    a. More impromptu
    b. More rehearsed

35. Do you get to the play
    a. Just in time
    b. Early

Preferences Assessment Scoring Sheet

Enter a check in the appropriate column for each question.

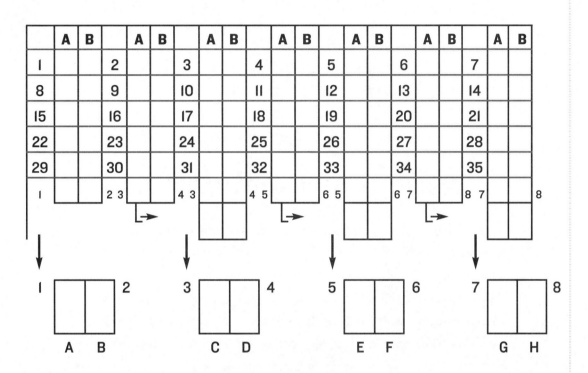

Directions for Scoring

Add down so that the total number of A answers is written in the box at the bottom of each column. Do the same for B answers.

Transfer the number in the first box above the answer grid to the box below the answer grid. Do this for the second box. Note, however, that all the subsequent rows have two columns. Bring down the first number for each box beneath the second, as indicated by the horizontal arrows. Add all of the pairs of numbers and enter the total in the boxes below the answer grid, so that each box has only one number.

Now you have four pairs of numbers. Circle the letter below the larger number of each. You now have identified your soliloquy:

CH—Soliloquy 1

CG—Soliloquy 2

DF—Soliloquy 3

DE—Soliloquy 4

Cast Your Leading Role

Each of the following soliloquies describes one distinct role and the characteristics that influence careers. Client stories follow to help clarify how obtaining a deeper understanding of your personality preferences brings greater clarity and direction to your career. Besides reading the soliloquy that matches your assessment results, you should also take a look at the other three soliloquies. Your corresponding soliloquy will be your primary role, but as we are all a mix of personalities, there may be other roles you identify with. It is important to understand these.

Soliloquy 1

I am impulse-driven.

I have The Creator value type.

I want to make an impact with my drive for action and results.

I like action, excitement, stimulation, and immediate adventure.

I perform with skill and can make a performance out of anything.

I value variety and have a talent for creating variations on a theme.

I troubleshoot, negotiate, and manage crisis well.

I am good with using tactics, interpreting situations, and making instant decisions.

I have the ability to vary something while keeping its essence the same.

I see the relevance of how things fit and notice when something is awry.

I prefer to learn in the applied context and do not like to learn in the abstract.

I often see opportunities others do not.

I want things to taste good, smell good, feel good, sound good, and look good.

I am spontaneous.

I love to entertain.

I am oriented to the here and now.

I improvise well, composing or performing on the spur of the moment.

I communicate best with stories because they entertain and have impact.

I exhibit the following qualities in my career:

Ability to solve problems

Practicality

Inclination to welcome change

Willingness to take risks

Acceptance of colleagues matter-of-factly

Flexibility

Open-mindedness

Natural talent for negotiating

Knack for lending excitement

I am happiest when working with equipment.

I am interested in all types of the arts, including the athletic, culinary, beauty, literary, martial, mechanical, rhetorical, theatrical, political, and industrial.

I possess skills in promoting, operating, displaying, and composing.

I like to be where the action is.

Sean is a client who represents this soliloquy well. Sean started his career as a cabinetmaker. He did not like traditional classroom learning, and while he liked school because he was popular and fun to have as a classmate, the only classes he accelerated in were woodworking and mechanics. Sean completed an apprentice program with one of the country's best furniture manufacturers and set out on a career making high-end customized cabinets.

About 7 years into his career, Sean married and began assessing his ability to provide for the needs of his family over the long term. He watched his friends rising in rank and compensation and decided he should pursue a career that would allow him to receive the stable salary and benefits a corporate job could offer. After closing his cabinet business, Sean went back to school to brush up on his business administration skills. He was particularly interested in learning how to use computer systems and technologies applicable to office management.

Upon completion of his classes, he secured a position as the office manager for a small psychology clinic. Sean played a significant role in managing the practice as it grew tenfold over the next 10 years and his salary tripled. When he started his career-counseling program, he spent the first session discussing all of the great aspects of his career, both as a cabinetmaker and as the office manager. While his decision was to pursue a complete career change from cabinetmaker to office administrator, he saw similarities in what motivated him and how he liked to work. He liked having a lot of variety. He liked crisis management and negotiating contracts with vendors. He enjoyed being the point person for the staff and ensuring that the systems he developed were processing information and data in an efficient manner. He was proud of the creative solutions he came up with that saved the practice time and money and liked having the authority to do what needed to be done without the clinic practitioners constantly looking over his shoulder. The personality preferences outlined in Soliloquy 1 were a direct match for Sean. He was an artist as a cabinetmaker, but he was also an artist in his ability to create a thriving practice for the psychologists. He took pride in both of his career paths.

After sharing all the positives, he began to explain why he was ready for a change. He was not challenged or excited to go to work anymore. After 10 years, he had lost his interest. Essentially, his ability to create and act on impulses was no longer needed. In the beginning, the company was growing and everything was new and stimulating. He was constantly developing relationships with clients, vendors, and staff. He trained the new employees and divided the company into departments. He selected the proprietary software and customized it to meet the specific needs of the practice. Sean played such a significant role in creating that office that he was confident in stating that he easily knew more about the company than anyone else, including the owners. Now, after 10 years, Sean felt stifled. Each day he stayed, the less useful he felt to the organization.

Sean is a creative person who needed to grow and be challenged, and the practice he had helped grow was maxed out, and the principals were not interested in getting any bigger. At first Sean thought that his distress at work was related to the industry. He had been passionate about woodworking and loved the art of cabinetmaking. He wondered if he had not made a huge mistake in leaving his trade years ago. After all, he had no passion for psychology. What Sean came to realize through his exploration and self-analysis is that the industry was not the issue so much as the stage of the company's life cycle. A mature company looking for someone to come in and maintain an office that is already well-established would be suffocating for Sean. He thrives in an environment that needs someone to wear multiple hats, be constantly learning and trying new business strategies, and developing relationships with key individuals both inside and outside the organization.

Sean appreciated and was equally appreciated for his ability to make quick decisions and perform beautifully in a fast-paced, sometimes chaotic environment. Upon realizing where his discontentment stemmed from, Sean identified start-up companies that needed a high-performing office manager and customized his résumé to articulate his accomplishments in managing fast growth in small businesses. Sean also recognized that he will probably not stay in just one position or one company for the rest of his life and that change is refreshing for him. This awareness made his search a welcome one because he understood the dynamics causing his dissatisfaction. As a result, he was able to articulate his reasons for pursuing advancement opportunities with prospective employers in a positive and growth-producing light. Sean completed his search by accepting a position with a high-tech service company that he found through his research of the *Inc.* 500 fastest-growing companies. In this company, he will be charged with creating a high-performance office. Sean did not have to stay a cabinetmaker to be creative and satisfied. He needed to understand his preferences so that he could create a career in alignment with his strengths.

Soliloquy 2

I have a strong need for affiliation.

I have The Maximizer value type.

I make sure that procedures are followed.

I am frequently given the authority to ensure production, quality, and productivity.

I facilitate and accommodate to support my team.

I prefer traditional ways of doing things.

I provide stability, making rules and enforcing them.

I appreciate consistency, predictability, and accountability.

I am interested in accurate measurement.

I naturally look at things in sequence.

I take pride in the ability to provide for others' comfort or material well-being.

I want to follow a defined chain of command.

I focus on cost-reduction efforts.

I like a structured sequence—a schedule, a beginning, and an end.

I can be counted on to follow through on commitments.

I notice when something is missing or not done right.

I am cautious and careful, relying on the past to know what to trust in the future.

I exhibit the following qualities in my career:

Stability

Confidence

Decisiveness

Orderliness

Dependability

Adherence to standards/structure/policies/procedures

Belief in giving rewards through promotions and bonuses

Conservation of corporate values

I like occupations that involve procedures for managing materials and services.

I am best suited to work that relies on standard operations and by-the-book procedures.

I find satisfaction in office work and administration.

I like keeping records, checking inventory, attending to correspondence, and accounting, as well as roles of executive, administrator, and office manager in commodities and finance.

I am a clear communicator and cooperative in implementing goals.

I am highly skilled in logistics.

I am skilled in supervising, inspecting, supplying, and protecting.

I like commerce, regulatory, and material work.

Seth is a client who sought a career-counseling program because his company and, by extension, the entire industry had been affected negatively by the economy. Seth, a 52-year-old facilities manager for a chemical-manufacturing plant in the Midwest, lost his job when his company downsized. He had been with the company for more than 17 years and identified himself as a company man. In every counseling session he attended, his shirt, jacket, or baseball cap adorned the company logo, as did his briefcase, portfolio, and pens. Seth considered himself good at his job but was quick to state that it was also a means to an end. He did not live to work but worked to live. At the same time, he struggled to come up with interests he held outside of work.

He was reliable and very thorough, and held pride in his ability to run a lean organization that experienced very little error and was recognized as a smooth operation that could be counted on. He explained that his wife called him predictable, but he liked it that way. Since his career had been at a chemical manufacturer, safety was a major area of importance, and he took it very seriously. Every policy and procedure was followed to a T. He served as the liaison between the Environmental Protection Agency (EPA) and the plant for regular safety visits.

Seth did not want a major career change. He wanted to find a position that would fulfill him for another 10 years. While he could retire if he wanted to, the thought of not working made both him and his wife deeply unsettled. After completing an extensive self-analysis, he decided that his career choices had been a good fit for him, and he would like to do something similar. He also decided that he was not willing to move at this stage in his life and so would pursue only positions that were local. There were no other chemical-manufacturing plants in the immediate area, and ones farther away were not hiring.

Seth decided his best option was to pursue career opportunities that required extensive knowledge and expertise in environmental safety. With this clarity, he was able to create a list of prospective companies as well as local, state, and federal regulatory agencies that would benefit from his experience. Seth customized his résumé to highlight his accomplishments around safety and environmental regulations, and within 4 months, he secured a position through a contact at the EPA with a large commercial airline company that had its industrial supplies shipping hub within a 40-mile commute from his home. One of the most beneficial aspects of conducting Seth's self-assessment was helping him see himself as separate from the company. He learned to recognize his expertise and talents as associated with a profession, not a company. This transformation played a significant role in helping him see a fit for himself in other companies that need help complying with environmental regulations.

Soliloquy 3

I am in search of the answer to the question "Who am I?"

I have The Humanitarian value type.

I place a high value on the "greater good."

I value cooperative interaction and empathetic relationships.

I develop others' potential.

I am an advocate, satisfied in information-giving roles.

I bring out the best in others.

I build bridges between people and help them to resolve conflicting issues.

I have a talent for explaining what is meant and see similarities across disparate categories.

I know what to say to help others help themselves.

I have an ability to recognize someone's deeper motivations and a talent for expressing that knowledge so he or she also knows it.

I am a facilitator, easing relationships between people.

I create harmony in relationships.

I engage in spiritual practices.

I am a natural giver of sincere compliments.

I am capable of seeing positive aspects that others miss.

I am impressionistic.

I focus on how others will feel in a given situation.

I inspire others to action.

I believe in the goodness in everyone, starting with faith first, skepticism second.

I develop metaphors easily and use language rich with them.

I exhibit the following qualities in my career:

Interpersonal focus

Natural optimism

Praise

Ability to bring out the best in others

Patience with complicated people issues

I am drawn to recruiting, training, mediating, advancing, teaching, and counseling.

I am excellent at finding quality employees for the right positions and helping them develop over the course of their careers.

I am naturally good at influencing the maturation of others.

I am highly skilled in diplomacy as well as educating and advising.

A client representing this particular soliloquy was a senior vice president of a regional bank in the Midwest. When I asked him to reflect on how the results from this assessment spoke to his career satisfaction or dissatisfaction, he said the following:

"Interestingly, my title and rank within my industry and profession do not reflect this soliloquy, but what has made me enjoy my work for more than 24 years is very clear in this description. You see, what I enjoy most about my career has been the opportunity to develop my team. I've been incredibly fortunate to have such wonderful people to help grow in their careers and become very successful leaders within the financial industry." I then asked him to explain how this description is carried out in his leadership style, and he said, "Well, it sounds cliché, but I have always treated my team as I want to be treated—as a unique person with a life that is centered around my family, community, and sense of purposefulness." When asked for an example, he said, "Well, when I say that I see my team as people first and employees second, what I mean is that I really know my team. I not only know them; I know who their spouses are and what their kids favorite sports are . . . their birthdays and anniversaries and personal victories and challenges. I know these things because I care about them as people and recognize that they, as we all are, are so much more than our 'jobs.' And because I know that and respect that, I have been fortunate to get so much more from them than any leader can ever ask. In fact, seven of my previous account executives not only consistently broke every corporate goal but have gone on to lead their own divisions to world-class status. They make me proud, and that pleases them more than any corporate incentive."

David was a client who by credentials alone would not have been identified with the personality preferences above. But from listening to him, it was clear that he most associated with these results because his career satisfaction is tied directly to the culture of the organization and leadership. When David began his career-counseling program, it was because he and his wife had decided to move to Denver to be closer to their children and grandchildren. David did not want to quit working completely but was ready to retire from the banking industry. The results of his assessments and personal exploration helped confirm his desire to pursue a retirement career in the nonprofit sector. He wanted to contribute in a meaningful way but on a broader scale. He received great reward from his accomplishments as a family man and inspirational leader to his sales team, but now he wanted his passion for developing others' potential to reach larger audiences. David's wife was already very involved in the nonprofit sector, and together they joined forces to support an early child-care education agency for working moms in Colorado.

Soliloquy 4

I possess willpower and self-control.

I have The Pursuer value type.

I solve abstract problems, conduct scientific research, and perform as an expert.

I seek objective knowledge, truth, concepts, and ideas.

I promote progress and scientific inquiry.

I gravitate to roles as an engineer or inventor.

I keep information flowing to make sure that every contingency is covered.

I am a perpetual learner.

I think way ahead of my time.

I am a strategist.

I analyze a situation abstractly and consider new possibilities.

I focus on theories and have a capacity to look at things from many different perspectives.

I am a perfectionist.

I come up with new and better ways of doing things.

I exhibit the following qualities in my career:

Vision

Intellectual curiosity

Skepticism

Economy

I am highly skilled in strategic analysis.

I am competent in action, autonomous, and strong-willed.

I like the sciences, technology, and systems-related work.

Robert is a client who represents this soliloquy. When he began his career-counseling program, he was a psychiatrist for a large state agency where he had been employed for more than 23 years. He conducted very thorough intake assessments, diagnosed clients, prescribed treatment plans, and counseled clients with severe mental disorders. He had been actively engaged in research, writing frequently for professional journals and presenting at annual conferences and regional professional meetings.

What prompted him to seek career counseling was the fact that his profession was experiencing significant cuts from changes in the insurance industry, and he had been feeling the pinch more each year. In addition to suffering financially, he was required to spend less time with patients and complete far more paperwork. Overall, he felt as though the quality of his work was compromised.

Robert was not alone in his concern about his profession and began to seek out others to inquire about their career changes. Some people had opted to open private practices, but Robert had no interest in running his own business. Others sought roles in education as professors and instructors. Robert liked giving presentations to his colleagues at professional conferences, but the thought of teaching students in a traditional academic environment had no appeal. Pursuing a research position was another option, but from his experience and investigation into the field, he felt certain that the politics involved would surely overwhelm him. Robert decided a complete career change was in order. The challenge was determining what career he would enjoy.

Robert had been a psychiatrist for his entire adult life, and the results of his assessments brought about interesting discussion regarding why he liked his career. He realized that he was drawn to psychiatry because he viewed the human mind as a brilliant and complex system. "We really are just a big chemistry set," he said with a smile. He was fascinated by systems and analyzing how things work. He liked diagnosing problems and using his intellect and expertise to administer solutions. His hobbies were not focused on human issues but instead on fixing electronics and making intricate plastic models from thousands of tiny pieces that had to be put together in complex formations. He liked fixing objects that were intellectually stimulating and required a high level of expertise.

With this realization, he began reading books and magazines that discussed careers in technology. He quickly homed in on occupations that required an understanding of how complex systems work and the architectures used to build networks for large companies. He was fascinated and excited by the possibilities that lay ahead. A career path emerged, and he enrolled in a technical college and obtained a mentor working within his field of choice to shadow one day a week. Before he completed his degree, the time he spent with his mentor led to a contract project with a large bank preparing for a merger that would require two totally incompatible computer systems to be networked together. Robert was like a kid in a candy shop. He worked day and night learning the networks and different systems, mostly pro bono, and by the time he earned his degree, the bank had extended him a full-time position in their technology department. Robert made a complete career change on one hand because he left psychiatry to pursue technology, but he was able to make this transition because he understood his personality preferences and what motivated him to be successful. With that knowledge and insight, his career path felt like a smooth, not rocky, progression.

Obviously, there are more than four types of people. For example, there is no soliloquy for The Driver value type. Go back through each soliloquy and identify those aspects that best describe what you might say, do, or think about yourself. Pull all those statements into one profile so that you have your own personal soliloquy. Feel free to add your own statements. This assessment is here to start you thinking about what is natural for you. While knowing who you are seems so simple, it is not something you probably think about on a regular basis. You just are who you are. But the truth is that you bring to this world a set of preferences and natural abilities that lend themselves to a particular type of work. If you are clear about these preferences and abilities, then you will have a good chance of choosing work that needs those very traits. In this way, you will choose work that does feel like play.

_____

_____

_____

_____

_____

_____

_____

_____

_____

_____

_____

_____

_____

_____

_____

Your Personality Preferences

To further explore your natural traits and characteristics, you will complete several exercises that more clearly define who you are. These exercises break down your overall preferences into smaller parts so you better understand why you gravitate to one career path over another. By knowing your personality prefer-

> *"The great aim of education is not knowledge but action."*
>
> —Herbert Spencer

ences, you can identify environments where you will be appreciated and will perform with great reviews. You will learn about the style of leadership and the type of work environment best suited for your play as well. Also, personality preferences offer insights regarding the strengths and talents you offer an employer.

Predicting Career Selection
Based on Your Personality

Just as people who are right-handed prefer using their right hand, people with preferences for certain personality traits like to be in environments where those traits are appreciated. Using the next exercise, you can determine what kind of work will likely be most rewarding to you.

Read the four statements below and check the statement that best reflects you.

1. _____ "Bottom-line," results-oriented person
2. _____ Drawn to opportunities for practical service to people
3. _____ Want to find and facilitate possibilities for people
4. _____ Drawn to opportunities for problem solving, analysis, and design

If you selected number 1, your most satisfying career choices will be work that is concrete in action and objective in decision making.

For example, this client might be drawn to careers in banking, applied science, law enforcement, production, construction, administration, or business because these require technical skills with facts and objects. Clients who select number 1 prefer occupations that rely on their practical and analytical skills.

If you selected number 2, your most satisfying career choices will be in work that offers tangible results that focus on helping people.

For example, this client might be drawn to careers in health care, community service, teaching, supervision, religious service, or sales in the service industry. Clients who select this choice tend to prefer occupations that allow them to meet the daily needs of people, and they prefer to do activities and tasks that require them to be sympathetic and friendly.

Mitch is a client whose career selection was significantly influenced by his preference for providing practical service to people. When Mitch began his career-counseling program, he was employed as a general manager within a large retail operation. He had started working as a customer service associate for the company while in college, and upon graduation he was offered a full-time position. He was not passionate about management as a profession or retail as an industry, but he observed his friends struggling to find jobs and decided it would be a good start.

Seven years after he accepted the general manager position, he was still doing the same job, and the weekend and holiday hours were beginning to drain him. His wife worked traditional business hours, and he was frequently called in to work the evening and weekend shifts when one of his staff would inevitably call in sick.

Through his self-analysis and exploration of preferences, he realized that he found satisfaction in helping others and liked that the feedback he received was immediate. But he wanted his life's work to be more meaningful than locating an item in the store or assisting a special-needs customer. While he was not particularly strong in school, he did like science and had thought at one time of becoming a doctor. But when he explored the pros and cons of pursuing this professional track, he decided that the years of training and financial commitment would be too much for him to risk at this stage of his life.

Instead he began exploring professions within the health care industry that required less training and financial investment but that would still prove very rewarding. He researched the Web sites of medical schools and analyzed master's degree programs offered in health care. He went to hospitals and medical clinics and sifted through their internal directories to identify occupations that he had not heard of before and looked them up on the Internet. His mother was a nurse and he knew enough from her experience that he was not interested in this particular track, but he spent time talking with her as well as the doctors she referred him to inquire about other, less obvious occupations within the medical community.

Armed with an enormous amount of new and exciting information, Mitch began a detailed pros-and-cons list of each occupation. He then talked with professionals in his top-choice areas. After conducting informational interviews and shadowing one professional, Mitch decided to go back to school for 2 years to study to become a perfusionist. In simple terms, this a specialist in the emergency room who maintains a heartbeat during emergency surgery. It is very physically demanding, and the hours are not traditional, but the compensation is near that of a physician and it is extremely rewarding work. Mitch would know immediately that he had helped save someone's life.

If you selected number 3, your most satisfying career choices will be focused on the future and have an impact on human development.

For example, this client might be drawn to careers in psychology, research, literature, art, music, academia, and sociology. Clients who select the third choice tend to prefer occupations that require them to be understanding and use their communication skills. Unlike the clients who selected the second statement, these individuals do not need to see tangible results on a daily basis as long as they know their efforts are directed at supporting the health and wellness of others.

If you selected number 4, your most satisfying career choices need to be focused on the future and involve shaping things. For example, this client might be drawn to careers in physical science, computers, law, engineering, technical work, research, or management. Clients who select the fourth statement tend to prefer occupations that use their abilities to develop theoretical concepts and use their logical and analytical thinking skills.

Stephanie is a client who selected this preference during her career-counseling program. She was recruited straight out of her small college in northeast Ohio to become a laboratory technician. She recalled being excited about the career path at first. She was a biology major and had no interest in continuing her education into graduate school. Her grades were good, and she received better pay than most of her classmates who graduated with degrees in engineering and computer science. Stephanie felt fortunate.

She sought career counseling 7 years into her career because she was experiencing burnout. The professional track she was on led nowhere, and she dejectedly observed her counterparts with 15 or more years of experience doing the same job functions they had done every day for the previous 14. She felt stir-crazy being in the same routine day after day, "locked in a lab," she exclaimed.

Through her personal assessment and introspection, Stephanie recognized that what she liked about her career was the ability to investigate, analyze, and determine appropriate recommendations based on careful review of objects. What she needed was variety. She wanted to be outdoors traveling to different places. She wanted more human interaction, but not sales. She did not want to go back for a graduate degree but was willing to complete required on-the-job training and learn a new profession. With this insight, she began exploring possible options that fit her criteria.

Shortly after creating her list of important factors, she narrowed in on the profession of claims adjuster within the insurance industry. While driving to work one day, she noticed the car beside her had its company logo identifying itself as an insurance company, and she remembered that a branch office was not far from her house. On her way home that day, she stopped in to inquire about the role of a claims adjuster and to find out what qualifications were required to pursue this profession. She made several contacts and continued to learn about other opportunities. Stephanie prepared her résumé in a format that drew direct correlations between her career in the lab and that of a claims adjuster and was offered a position within 3 months. For Stephanie, the hardest part was envisioning how her talents could be used outside of her narrowly defined profession in the laboratory. Once she was able to identify the criteria that drove her decisions, she began to see all the options that had not been on her radar screen in the past.

Which of the above best describes you?

_____

_____

_____

Preferences not only help pinpoint the type of career you should select; they are also useful in helping you assess what is the best work environment for you.

Assessing Work Environments Based on Your Personality

Read the four statements below and check the statement that best reflects you.

1. _____ Persevering; change requires evidence that fits your perception.

2. _____ Introspective; adaptable to little things and firm on issues important to you.

3. _____ Active, energetic, sociable; deal with change readily and seek new experiences.

4. _____ Fast moving, confident, decisive; enjoy making things happen.

If you selected number 1, your most satisfying work environments need to have structure that does not easily move off course from core business objectives. For example, clients who select this statement tend to prefer environments that are steeped in history and tradition. It is the organization's depth of experience that gives it stability. These work environments tend to have a formal approach to managing business already in place, including set policies and procedures that everyone is held accountable for following.

If you selected number 2, your most satisfying work environments need to allow concentration on critical functions of the organization and flexibility regarding less important things. Clients who select this statement tend to prefer organizations that have carved out a niche for themselves and are highly specialized. The organizational structure may be flat instead of hierarchical, but the role of each individual is clear as a result of the different functions required by certain levels of education and expertise.

If you selected number 3, your most satisfying work environments need to be active and open to change. Clients who select the third statement are typically drawn to environments that are entrepreneurial and allow them to play a significant role in shaping the culture. They typically prefer smaller organizations that require them to wear a lot of hats. A start-up organization that encourages them to put their thumbprint into the business is a good fit for this personality.

If you selected number 4, your most satisfying work environments need to be active and driven toward an end that brings value to the organization. Clients who select this statement are drawn to environments that promote friendly competition among peers and reward their associates based on performance. People must be highly recognized for their contributions and praised for the value they offer.

Using the information above, describe your ideal work environment.

_____

_____

_____

Now you know what environment is a good fit for your preferences. But what about the kind of leadership style under which you will perform best?

The next exercise examines your own leadership style and the leadership style you most appreciate in others.

Assessing Your Preferred Leadership Style Based on Your Personality

You can also learn about the most appropriate leadership style from your personality preferences. Read the four statements below and select the statement that best describes your preferred leadership style.

1. _____ Tough-minded, analytical, and an instrumental leader. These leaders make decisions based on principles and systems, overall impact, and rational analysis of outcomes.

2. _____ Objective, skeptical, and curious, especially about materials and possibilities. These leaders create consistent and orderly frameworks for understanding and leading.

3. _____ Adaptable, seek harmony and affiliation, and concerned with the human aspects of problems. These leaders lead by encouragement and coaching.

4. _____ Observant about people and their needs, bringing harmony into relationships. These leaders make decisions based on personal values and identification with others. They are expressive leaders who inspire and teach others.

If you selected number 1, your preferred leadership style is objective and decisive. You place most value on leaders who are fair and consistent. You have little respect for leaders who show favoritism or change their minds at a moment's notice without clear explanation. You want a leader who does things "by the book."

If you selected number 2, your preferred leadership style is one that is open to new growth. You appreciate leaders who do not struggle with difficult decisions, particularly when it comes to their employees. You want a leader who is strict about following the rules but is also open to new ideas for making the organization more efficient, productive, and profitable.

If you selected number 3, your preferred leadership style is warm, person-centered, and adaptable. You appreciate leaders who embrace their employees as unique individuals first and workers second. While these leaders sometimes struggle with making difficult decisions regarding employees, they take each situation separately and analyze it to determine the best solution given the circumstances. These are leaders who create a "family" environment at work.

If you selected number 4, your preferred leadership style is person-centered and structured in a way that produces vehicles for teaching others. You appreciate leaders who are committed to promoting from within. These leaders recognize themselves as the figurehead of the organization and use their passion and enthusiasm to motivate others.

Using the information above, describe your preferred leadership style.

_____

_____

_____

The final portion of this section on preferences examines the strengths you are likely to exhibit and therefore should be using in your work.

Applying Strengths to Your Career

To identify which preferences you exercise on a regular basis, and which therefore are likely to become your strengths, read the statements in Group 1 and Group 2 and select which group best describes how you understand the world around you.

GROUP I

- You prefer a past-to-present orientation, and you tend to scan back through stored data to find relevant experiences and apply it to new information.
- You focus on work at hand.
- You like detailed and clear instructions that produce tangible results.

Clients who choose Group 1 tend to be good with facts and details. They approach their work in a sequential manner and look for the most practical solution to complete a task.

GROUP 2

- You prefer a present-to-future orientation, and you scan ahead to open many possibilities and generate new ideas.
- You prefer to focus on several things at once.
- You like to figure out how things work and are intrigued by possibilities and future implications.

Clients who choose Group 2 tend to think about all possibilities and are typically seen as visionaries rather than implementers. They are likely to go by their hunches and are able to see patterns and connections between two seemingly unrelated concepts.

Which group of statements best describes you?

Group 1   or   Group 2

It is perfectly acceptable to have preferences in both Groups 1 and 2; many people do. The goal of this exercise is to understand which group is more natural for you. The objective is to use this information to clearly identify what strengths are likely to emerge as a result of your preferences. Next read the statements in Group 3 and Group 4 to determine which is more natural for you when making decisions and interacting with others.

GROUP 3

- You have an objective approach to decision making that is detached and based on logic developed by established principles and policies.

- You tend to be calm and approach disagreements as a form of information sharing.

- You manage conflict resolution in a matter-of-fact manner, focusing on the logic formed from policies and principles held by the organization.

Clients who select Group 3 tend to rely most heavily on their rational thinking skills to come to conclusions. They prefer to use facts to justify an action, instead of persuasive acumen. They are more comfortable stepping back from a situation and analyzing it without letting their own personal perspective influence their decisions.

GROUP 4

- You have a subjective approach to decision making that is based on your personal values and your understanding of how you experience the specific situation.

- You tend to focus on people's feelings and prefer harmony over objectivity in resolving conflicts.

- You are stressed by disagreements and use your personal experiences and values as a means of determining the outcome.

Clients that select Group 4 are more likely to have their heartstrings pulled than others. They are deeply influenced by their emotions and have a gift for empathizing with, and seeing good in, others that is lost to their counterparts.

Sara's career choice was deeply impacted by her assessing her strengths and learning about her natural approach to decision making. Sara had spent 15 years as an attorney with a medium-size law firm that specialized in business law. Sara contacted me because she hated her job and did not want to get up in the morning to go to work. She wanted to make a change and she wanted to make it fast. As part of her career exploration process, she reviewed her personality preferences and strengths. Upon reviewing her results, she was stunned to realize that her natural preference in decision making is to be heavily subjective and go with her feelings and gut instincts. This contrasted sharply with the profession she had chosen, which required detailed and objective analysis of the facts and law. Sara also had a Humanitarian value type and very much wanted to feel she was contributing to her clients' happiness and well-being. Working with businesses on contract issues just didn't seem to fulfill this need. As an interim step, Sara began volunteering in her spare time at a local legal assistance foundation for the poor, helping to make "equal justice under the law" a reality. She is making a gradual shift in her career priorities, with her ultimate goal to work as a public defender.

Which group of statements best describes you?

Group 3   or   Group 4

Reread the two groups you have selected and choose the one that you feel dominates your personality style. For example, if a best friend was asked to describe you, which group would be emphasized as a dominant characteristic of you?

Pick the group (1 through 4) that resonates most with you.

Group _____

Now that you have identified the group that you associate the strongest with, read the statement below that follows it. Your selection should describe your greatest natural strength.

Group 1: You are unparalleled at remembering facts and putting them to good use. You possess superior attention to detail, are able to document minute changes, and have outstanding accuracy.

Group 2: You are able to see connections and implications that no one else does. You show natural creativity and influence others with your vision.

Group 3: You are without equal when it comes to making objective analyses. You have an excellent ability to evaluate the logical effects of different strategic moves and then choose an approach decisively and calmly.

Group 4: You are able to evaluate situations in human terms. You show outstanding relationship management, client advocacy, and customer service.

After reviewing each of the statements above, select the preference strength that best describes you and write it in the space provided below. Then, describe in more detail your greatest strength.

_____

_____

_____

_____

_____

Your greatest natural strengths tend to evolve into your talents. Next you will examine what talents should be included in your repertoire of assets that serve as the template for writing your script—the résumé that achieves the goal of communicating to employers what makes you a valuable and satisfied performer.

Talents

Talents are highly developed personality traits and characteristics. Talents come naturally and are perfected through training, discipline, and access to environments that encourage their development. Your true talents may be the very elements of yourself most overlooked and taken for granted. This is because your greatest gifts come naturally, so it is sometimes difficult to recognize them as special or unique. It is important that an organization uses your best talents. The following assessment helps you identify your talents to ensure they become a conscious part of your Leading Role.

TALENTS ASSESSMENT

Identifying your talents begins by observing yourself and selecting experiences in your life where you felt centered or natural. To begin this process, read through the following statements and jot down activities, events, places, people, and things that come to mind. You do not have to respond to every statement. Only respond to statements that invoke a memory and help you think about your natural talents.

Name a time in your life when you felt:

- Energized by the challenge
- It was difficult to distract you
- Absorbed by what you were doing
- Mesmerized
- You lost track of time
- You did not want to be interrupted or disrupted

- The activity was worthwhile and valuable

- This was a good use of time

- It might not be important to anyone else, but it was to you

- Peace and serenity

- Energized instead of drained

- You had total patience with this activity

- You had tapped into a source of knowledge

- There was a naturalness about this

- When this was finished, there was self-appreciation

- A calling

- You could not wait to have the experience again

- You were growing

- You could not believe you got paid to do it

- No one taught you how to do this; it just came naturally

- Spiritual

- A sense of accomplishment

- You were proud of your work

- This was fun

- In harmony

- Engrossed by the challenge

- You had the ability to think very quickly and clearly

Review the answers and prioritize below the top five talents you possess; these are the talents that are most important to you.

Your Top Five Talents

1. _____

2. _____

3. _____

4. _____

5. _____

Now you have deepened your understanding of your natural talents and strengths that are most likely to produce career satisfaction for you. You also know the types of careers, work environments, and leadership styles that fit you most comfortably. These are valuable assets as you move to the next phase of the play of your life. The process of finding yourself center stage requires not only a clear understanding of how your values and personality preferences impact your career choices but also an awareness of your interests and fascinations. In the next chapter, you will integrate into the fold new information about the subjects, hobbies, activities, and places you appreciate. You will also be challenged to take the basic interest and fascination results from the inventories and use them to create new ideas and options for yourself. In the play of your life, your career choices must keep your attention over time and be interesting to you.

The Plot

SO FAR YOU have examined your values, personality preferences, and talents. Now you will add to the mix an exploration of your interests and fascinations. Knowing your interests and fascinations is important because they represent activities and subjects that hold your attention over time. Just as you probably prefer to see plays that have interesting plots, it is likely that you would prefer to engage in a profession that focuses on a product or service that has some interest to you. If you know what interests you, then it will be easier to identify careers that speak to those interests.

> *"To find out what one is fitted to do and to secure an opportunity to do it is the key to happiness."*
>
> —*John Dewey*

In creating the play of your life, you need to develop a plot that holds your attention over time and is meaningful to you. To help you learn more, you will take several assessments designed to prioritize and clarify your interests and fascinations. After completing an interests assessment and fascinations assessment, you will use the results in several brainstorming exercises, which expand beyond the obvious interests and fascinations in a way that opens your mind to new possibilities.

The following exercise is designed to help you learn about the interest profiles that best fit you.

INTERESTS ASSESSMENT

Directions: Circle the numbers of the statements that clearly feel like something you might say or do or think—something that feels like you.

1. It is important for me to be physically fit and in excellent condition.
2. I need to understand things thoroughly.
3. Music, color, and beauty of any kind can really affect my moods.
4. People enrich my life and give it meaning.
5. I have confidence in myself that I can make things happen.
6. I appreciate clear directions so I know exactly what to do.
7. I can usually carry/build/fix things myself.
8. I can get absorbed for hours in thinking something out.
9. I appreciate beautiful surroundings; color and design mean a lot to me.
10. I love company.
11. I enjoy competing.
12. I need to get my surroundings in order before I start a project.
13. I enjoy making things with my hands.
14. It is satisfying to explore new ideas.

15. I always seem to be looking for new ways to express my creativity.

16. I value being able to share personal concerns with people.

17. Being a key person in a group is very satisfying to me.

18. I take pride in being very careful about all the details of my work.

19. I do not mind getting my hands dirty.

20. I see education as a lifelong process of developing and sharpening my mind.

21. I love to dress in unusual ways, to try new colors and styles.

22. I can often sense when a person needs to talk to someone.

23. I enjoy getting people organized and on the move.

24. A good routine helps me get the job done.

25. I like to buy sensible things I can make or work on myself.

26. Sometimes I can sit for long periods of time and work on puzzles, read, or just think about life.

27. I have a great imagination.

28. It makes me feel good to take care of people.

29. I like to have people rely on me to get the job done.

30. I am satisfied knowing that I have done an assignment carefully and completely.

31. I would rather be on my own, doing practical, hands-on activities.

32. I am eager to read about any subject that arouses my curiosity.

33. I love to try creative new ideas.

34. If I have a problem with someone, I prefer to talk it out and resolve it.

35. To be successful, it is important to aim high.

36. I prefer being in a position where I do not have to take responsibility for decisions.

37. I do not enjoy spending a lot of time discussing things. What is right is right.

38. I need to analyze a problem pretty thoroughly before I act on it.

39. I like to rearrange my surroundings to make them unique and different.
40. When I feel down, I find a friend to talk to.
41. After I suggest a plan, I prefer to let others take care of the details.
42. I am usually content where I am.
43. It is invigorating to do things outdoors.
44. I keep asking "why."
45. I like my work to be an expression of my moods and feelings.
46. I like to find ways to help people care more for each other.
47. It is exciting to take part in an important decision.
48. I am always glad to have someone else take charge.
49. I like my surroundings to be plain and practical.
50. I need to stay with a problem until I figure out an answer.
51. The beauty of nature touches something deep inside me.
52. Close relationships are important to me.
53. Promotion and advancement are important to me.
54. Efficiency, for me, means doing a set amount carefully each day.
55. A strong system of law and order is important to me.
56. Thought-provoking books always broaden my perspective.
57. I look forward to seeing art shows, plays, and good films.
58. I have not seen you for so long; I'd love to know how you are doing.
59. It is exciting to influence people.
60. When I say I will do it, I follow through on every detail.
61. Good, hard physical work never hurt anyone.
62. I would like to learn all there is to know about subjects that interest me.
63. I do not want to be like everyone else; I like to do things differently.
64. Tell me how I can help you.
65. I am willing to take some risks to get ahead.

66. I like exact directions and clear rules when I start something new.
67. The first thing I look for in a car is a well-built engine.
68. Those people are intellectually stimulating.
69. When I create, I tend to let everything else go.
70. I feel concerned that so many people in our society need help.
71. It is fun to get ideas across to people.
72. I hate it when they keep changing the system just when I get it down.
73. I usually know how to take care of things in an emergency.
74. Just reading about those new discoveries is exciting.
75. I like to create happenings.
76. I often go out of my way to pay attention to people who seem lonely and friendless.
77. I love to bargain.
78. I do not like to do things unless I'm sure they're approved.
79. Sports are important in building strong bodies.
80. I have always been curious about the way nature works.
81. It is fun to be in a mood to try or do something unusual.
82. I believe that people are basically good.
83. If I do not make it the first time, I usually bounce back with energy and enthusiasm.
84. I appreciate knowing exactly what people expect of me.
85. I like to take things apart to see if I can fix them.
86. Do not get excited. We can think it out and plan the right move logically.
87. It would be hard to imagine my life without beauty around me.
88. People often tell me their problems.
89. I can usually connect with people who get in touch with a network of resources.
90. I do not need much to be happy.

Score Your Answers

To score, circle the same numbers below that you circled on the test.

T	S	C	H	B	L
1	2	3	4	5	6
7	8	9	10	11	12
13	14	15	16	17	18
19	20	21	22	23	24
25	26	27	28	29	30
31	32	33	34	35	36
37	38	39	40	41	42
43	44	45	46	47	48
49	50	51	52	53	54
55	56	57	58	59	60
61	62	63	64	65	66
67	68	69	70	71	72
73	74	75	76	77	78
79	80	81	82	83	84
85	86	87	88	89	90

Now add up the number of circles in each column:

T	S	C	H	B	L

Which are your three highest scores?

1st	
2nd	
3rd	

Interest Descriptions

After you identify your top three categories, read their definitions to see how well they describe you.

Tangible (T)

- You seek practical accomplishments and appreciate rules.

- You are frank, self-reliant, and productive; are concrete in your thinking style; and are a strong individual.

- You are drawn to occupations that involve building, growing, or repairing, and using machines, tools, materials, and equipment.

- You possess good mechanical skills and like working with objects.

Clients with a Tangible profile rely on common sense, craftsmanship, and tradition to drive their occupational choices. They are productive in environments that are organized, structured, and product-driven and that offer clear lines of authority. Tangible types enjoy solving concrete problems, fixing things, and using equipment that requires coordination and mechanical dexterity. Occupations they are drawn to include transportation, manufacturing, engineering, energy, construction, and protective services.

Dean is a good example of the Tangible profile. He possesses a degree in horticulture and landscape design from a notable university. Dean put himself through college and bought his first car and first home through a lawn care business that he started in high school and ran until he was 22. He really enjoyed those years and looks back on them fondly. Since then he has been in five different companies in 8 years, each one more unfulfilling than the one before. The companies he worked for had several commonalities. They were all small companies with a flat organizational chart. They all seemed to be changing their focus frequently, and they all looked to Dean to be the leader for new ideas and business development. Dean had gotten used to being well-compensated and had run his own company, so applying for jobs that made him the primary businessperson had made great sense to him. The problem was that he was not working in the profession anymore. He was working on the business and constantly needed to change and adapt to new business plans from the owners.

After a thorough analysis of his likes and dislikes and with a clear understanding of his interests, Dean realized that he was in the right industry but not in the right profession or company. He began researching the largest real-estate development firms in the country, as well as city, state, and federal urban-planning and development departments. In this regard, he was able to secure a stable position with a clear hierarchical chain of command and perform tasks that allowed him to get his hands back into design. Dean accepted a landscape design position with a large commercial real-estate development firm that was awarded most contracts for building arenas around the country. Dean's specific responsibility is for the structural layout and designs of parking lots and the landscaping around the new arenas. For Dean, this position is perfect. It is clearly defined and tangible, and it allows him to work on projects that are interesting to him.

Scientific (S)

- You like to analyze objects, using your highly developed independent thinking skills to create new knowledge or use existing knowledge.
- You are technically proficient and oriented toward science.
- You have strong academic skills and are seen by others as scholarly and often introverted.

Clients with a Scientific profile tend to rely on their intellectual and critical-thinking skills to perform their work. They are more naturally reserved and introspective in their approaches to solving problems and use their curiosity to drive original and complex developments. They prefer occupations that are knowledge-based and value innovative thinking and abstract mental challenges. For example, these clients might thrive in higher education, research, medicine, science, computer industries, and engineering/design fields. They like to collect and organize data that is used to solve intellectually stimulating problems.

Scott was a client with a high Science profile. He pursued science into postgraduate school but stopped prior to obtaining his doctoral degree when he and his wife had their first baby and financial pressures required him to secure stable employment. With his master's degree in chemistry and postgraduate research work on his side, he set out to join corporate America and secured a position with a company that manufactures specialty instruments used in high-precision scales.

Scott rose quickly through the ranks in the company and was promoted to marketing director a year and half before starting his career-counseling program. The problem he faced was that he did not like marketing or sales. He wanted the compensation increase, which required him to leave the lab, and he liked the idea of working on new product launches, but for the last 18 months he had been traveling extensively, selling commodity products in a highly competitive and saturated market. He was deeply dissatisfied.

While Scott felt regret for not having completed his Ph.D.—which would have opened the opportunity to pursue his original career goal, a professorship at the university—he knew that returning to that track presented significant hurdles. His family had grown from one to four children, and he was the sole income provider. As such, he felt staying within the corporate landscape was the best choice for him at this stage in his career. But at age 45, he did not want to work for 20 more years as a "dumb sales guy," an expression he used frequently in his counseling sessions.

Through his self-analysis, he realized that what he enjoyed is the emerging technologies in his profession. Even his research studies as a doctoral student had been cutting-edge. He liked being an expert on a subject that few knew a lot about and educating others as to the power and purpose of this new finding or invention. When he was talking about a new, highly sophisticated product in a niche market, Scott's ability to motivate buyers and grow the company was outstanding.

He began to identify related companies throughout the Midwest and Northeast that were receiving at least $5 million from venture capitalists. He also identified companies that had been recently spun off from larger corporations to penetrate a niche market with a new product. Scott conducted a very narrow and in-depth search process that was extremely focused. This made his career search easier because it was more in alignment with his personality style and temperament. Scott identified a company that was ideal for him and approached them to serve as the liaison between sales/marketing and the new-product development team in the lab. While it took him 8 months of networking to finally secure a position, he made a transition that was far less frustrating than for similar people who conduct traditional job searches.

Creative (C)

- You are artistic, imaginative, and innovative.
- You like to use your creativity to express feelings and emotions.
- You are drawn to the arts, performance, writing, and fields that appreciate unusual ideas and aesthetic styles.

Clients with a high Creative profile gravitate to occupations that appreciate free-spirited and original thinkers. They are unconventional and intense, preferring to create a new path rather than follow traditional norms. They prefer creative work that allows a lot of independence and opportunity to change things. Occupations include professions in advertising, fine arts, interior design, photography, dramatics, and music.

Jill is a good example of a client with a high Creative profile. When she began her career-counseling program, she had recently completed her fine arts degree in photography from a large state university. She had been supporting herself through a paid position at a local photography studio that specialized in family portraits, local weddings, and other traditional photo shoots. She felt disenchanted because all the positions she applied for were lacking in creativity. She had worked for a one-hour photo processing center, a high-end camera supply store, a commercial photography house that supplied mostly stock photos to advertising agencies, and now this small suburban studio. Needless to say, Jill was suffocating. She desperately wanted to use her talent in photography, but in a more meaningful and creative way. She also felt stifled in her hometown.

One day, as Jill was waiting for her counseling appointment, she noticed a business card of one of the office building's tenants, an art therapist. During our appointment, Jill inquired about the profession. We talked about art therapy and explored resources available on the Internet for her to continue her research. Jill went to the library and checked out every book on the subject. She engaged in informational interviews with the art therapist in my building and with six others in differing specialties within art therapy. Next, Jill volunteered at the local children's hospital in a unit for abused children that uses art therapy as a principal means of counseling. She realized that she could use her love for photography in a creative way that encourages children and teenagers to express themselves. With her passion ignited, Jill applied to the art therapy graduate program at the University of Chicago. Jill got out of her hometown, is studying at one of the best art therapy schools in the country, and is customizing the program to incorporate photography. Like Jill, Creative types are frequently required to take a self-directed approach to finding their true fit. Because they are driven to creative fields, their ideal opportunities are less likely to be openly posted in the Sunday classifieds or by an Internet job search engine.

Human Development (H)

- You like to express feelings and emotions that directly impact people in a positive way.

- You are drawn to opportunities to teach, cure, help, counsel, train, minister, or support people.

- You are agreeable, patient, and outgoing, with highly developed social skills.

Clients with a high Human Development profile gravitate to environments that are cooperative and friendly. They want to motivate others, value consensus building and open communication, and work hard to create cultures that are supportive and comfortable for all associates. Occupations include careers in human resources, recreational services, education, religion, health services, child care, elderly care, and mental health.

Shelly is a good example of the Human Development profile. When she began her career-counseling program, she was an environmental engineer for a large corporate think tank in the Midwest. She knew she was not in a work culture that met her desire to be talkative and friendly and meet new people. The best part of her day was the dancing and gymnastics classes she took for fun after work. She also loved being a teacher for a children's tumbling class on weekends.

Shelly wanted a complete career change but also recognized that she held the role of primary income provider in her marriage, since her husband was a full-time doctoral student. Making an adequate living as a gymnastics teacher for children was not possible, and she was not physically able to become a paid dancer or gymnast. What Shelly chose to do combined her love of dance and helping children exercise with her excellent ability to excite others and make a positive difference in their lives. Here is how it happened!

Prior to becoming an environmental engineer, Shelly had worked in a mom-and-pop candy store to help fund her tuition expenses during college. For years afterward, she would frequently work there during holidays and when the store had rush orders. One day, a sales representative from Nestlé came into the store, and the owner asked about the representative's large order. The representative explained that she was the regional director who works with local cheerleading teams and sports teams to sell candy bars and chocolates as fund-raisers for their activities. The owner told her about Shelly, and an introduction followed shortly thereafter. Shelly is now a sales representative for Nestlé, making twice her income as when she was an engineer and using her talents in a field that helps support the activities she loves. Shelly used her insights about her personal interests and talents to forge a career path that is in alignment with who she is and what she likes to do.

Business (B)

- You like to lead, influence, direct, or manage people for organizational goals or economic gain.
- You appreciate status and power and are highly driven to attain leadership roles in business or politics.

Clients with a high Business profile seek adventurous opportunities that exercise their assertive and risk-taking qualities. They do not shy away from competitive environments and, in fact, often thrive in leadership roles that require them to influence and persuade others. They prefer debating ideas, selling/purchasing products, managing people/projects, entertaining clients, and giving presentations, as opposed to performing functions that require a high level of concentration and attention to minute details. Occupations that lend themselves well to the Business profile include sales, politics, fundraising, entrepreneurship, industry/manufacturing, and government.

Steve is a good example of client with a high Business profile. When Steve began his career-counseling program, he showed great pride in his credentials and successes to date. A graduate of an executive MBA program, associate partner with a world-class consulting firm, and recipient of many other accolades to support his highly developed business acumen, Steve was ready to take on the world. A major change in his personal life, however, prompted him to rethink his career choices.

Steve recently married his third wife and was about to have a child. At age 46, having missed the bulk of the child-rearing years of his children from previous marriages, he knew that the aggressive travel schedule and time demands needed to change if he did not want to repeat the past. The challenge was that while a significant part of him wanted his new family to come first, Steve could not get excited about any company that was not a Fortune 500, any position that was not a senior director level or higher, or any compensation under the mid-six-figure range. Steve said he needed to be home more but did not want to redefine his priorities. The money, title, prestige, travel, connections, and perks all made Steve feel important and defined success for him. At the time he began his career-counseling program, he did not realize how powerful his need was for status and financial reward. He did not fully know what defined success for him and what motivations prompted his choices. When he decided to make a career change, he became discouraged quickly.

Through extensive self-analysis and a thorough exploration of who he is and what he wants, he was able to better understand why he was so disappointed with the alternative options ahead of him. This was important because for the first time Steve actually came to know himself and in doing so was able to make the decision to change his priorities and redefine success for himself. Only then could he find attraction in his career alternatives.

Steve gave himself permission to measure success by the amount of time he spent with his family and his ability to make an impact on a local company. Steve still pursued highly visible roles in sales for companies with glamorous products and services. These are factors that motivate and provide interest for Steve, but he was able to do so within a framework that adjusted to his new commitment to family and community. Steve realized that saying you want a change and actually making a change can be worlds apart, especially if you do not know the source of your true motivations and needs.

Logistical (L)

- You appreciate organizational efficiency and task completion.
- You prefer to execute and manage a process, as opposed to people.
- You are a great organizer and stabilizer within companies and enjoy clearly defined rules and established structures for getting things done.

Clients with a high Logistical profile are drawn to work that requires precision, accuracy, and systematic approaches. They are practical and dependable and use these strengths to create stability and security within organizations. Logistical profiles are more patient and prudent than the other profiles and are excellent with keeping records, writing business reports, making charts/graphs, and managing data and numbers. They are drawn to occupations in banking, finance, accounting, quality control, administration, government service, court reporting, and office management.

Jane is a good example of a Logistical profile. She is an accountant by training and has worked as an auditor for large public-school systems throughout a multistate region. While she has changed accounting firms every 2 to 3 years to find a better corporate culture for herself, she has been doing essentially the same job for more than 15 years. When I asked Jane about her interests, she explained that she loves computer programming and has taken a few courses at the local community college but is primarily self-taught through books and online guides and tutorials. When she started her career-counseling program, she explained that she was no longer satisfied in accounting and had not been for some time. She thought it might just be the wrong company, but after multiple lateral moves to new companies, she knows it is the profession. She also realized that she did not like working for an accounting firm business structure that requires her to support lots of clients, instead of working as an accountant for one company. In working for one company, she would be responsible for just their accounting and could become a true expert, rather than jumping from client to client. She did not enjoy the consulting engagement that required her to become an expert for several intense weeks, offer advice and make recommendations, and then be off to the next company.

Jane first decided to interview with companies looking for an in-house accountant, thinking that this would be an easier career shift than a full career change into a programming position. After multiple interviews with no offers extended, she realized that her lack of passion for accounting was causing her interviews to suffer. Jane decided she had to make the change if she was going to be happy in her career and enrolled at a local technical school to earn an accelerated programming degree. Jane completed her courses ahead of schedule and achieved straight A's.

Feeling gun-shy after her negative accounting interviews, Jane decided to interview for entry-level programming positions within the finance industry.

Her background as an accountant and new programming skills made an attractive combination. Jane identified companies that used a specific accounting software that she was well-versed in and began contacting each company to inquire about technical support/programmer positions. She landed a position at a large state-funded organization that was in the midst of a huge project, converting from an antiquated system to a new software program that Jane had spent countless hours supporting for previous employers.

It was a perfect fit, and her interview went extremely well because she was passionate about the profession and confident with her industry knowledge. Also, this move allowed her to stay away from consulting companies that hire programmers and place them in different client sites for intense short durations. Jane already knew from her experience that this was not a culture that fit her preferred style of performance.

Based on these interest descriptions, are the three interests from the assessment the ones that describe you best? If not, add additional information from the other interests.

By knowing your specific interests, you can develop a career path that is satisfying to you. Now you have a greater awareness of what environments, activities, and people are important elements of the career you seek.

Understanding Interests

The results from your interests assessment are important in determining how to best explore the marketplace. For example, your scores may show that you have interests in all of the profile areas or that you have interest in only one profile area. Your scores may show that you have interest profiles that appear to conflict with each other (for example, H—I like to help people, and T—I like to build things). The following sections offer suggestions on how to explore occupations based on the kind of results you rendered. For instance, if your results show a profile where interests do not seem related to one another and even appear to conflict with one another, here are several suggestions.

1. Identify occupations in one interest category that can be performed in an environment of another interest category. For example, if you are both Creative and Logistical, you may want to explore a role as a graphic designer (Creative) in a government agency (Logistical) or a role as an accountant (Logistical) for a large advertising agency (Creative).

2. Combine a vocation in one interest area with an avocation or hobby in another interest area. For example, if your results show interest in both a Tangible profile and Human Development profile, you may want to establish your profession in the construction industry (Tangible) and become a volunteer at a local hospice (Human Development). If your interests are Business and Scientific, you may work as a corporate executive (Business) but also run the local inventors' club (Scientific).

3. Consider consulting or contract work that allows you to spend time exercising both interest areas at different times. Be open to regular career changes, which can also produce satisfaction.

If your interests appear equal in many or all areas, it could suggest that you may want to keep all of your options open. It could also suggest that you unconsciously equate "disliking" an activity with being negative. If you circled every statement in the interests assessment, you may be indecisive or simply uncomfortable making judgments about whether you like something or not. Perhaps you prefer to err on the side of liking everything and indicate equal interest across all areas. The reverse can also happen if you choose not to circle any of the statements until you have more exposure to the various topics of all the statements. Of course, another reason for equal interests across all themes is a true diversity of interests.

If your results showed that your interest profiles were equal:

1. Identify career options that offer a wide variety of experiences and frequent changes.
2. Design your career progression to include numerous options that allow you to change direction every few years.
3. Establish a consulting practice that allows you to work on many different projects over time.
4. Explore an entrepreneurial route that typically requires you to wear many different hats.

Understanding Isolated Interests

If one interest profile is very strong and the others held little interest for you, then identify career options that focus on that interest area. Brainstorming exercises need to be focused on depth, not breadth. Look for books on this specific career area.

Expanding Occupational Choices

While looking in books to identify occupations of interest, important options may be missing from these resources because today's career landscape is full of emerging opportunities. Take, for example, the vinyl record industry. In 1985, this was a $2 billion industry that employed well over 100,000 people. By 1990, vinyl records were virtually obsolete as they were replaced by CDs. Now the music industry is undergoing another dramatic shift with the emergence of technology that allows consumers to download music from the Internet. Today's career-savvy clients are defined by their abilities to be adaptable to new information and technology. This way, as the industry changes, they are able to retool and capitalize on the new opportunities that emerge during these changes. New careers are opening in information and professional service occupations such as financial services, biotechnology, and aerospace.

The technology explosion has made a huge impact on the marketplace. Predictions have been made that 90 percent of all white-collar jobs in the United States will be altered beyond recognition or totally reinvented in the next 10 years. It is also estimated that 80 percent of the jobs in the United States in the next 20 years will be cerebral and only 20 percent manual, the exact opposite of the ratio in 1900. In fact, the Department of Labor states that 44 percent of all workers will soon be in data services—either gathering, processing, retrieving, or analyzing information.

Books that list occupations are a good resource for generating an initial list of occupations. However, this list should be expanded through creative brainstorming exercises. Generate new career opportunities for yourself in the following ways.

1. Develop a list of traditional occupations. Review each occupation, envisioning what a person in this occupation will do 10 years from now or even 100 years from now. Write down careers and occupations that come to mind.
2. Write down the opposite of each occupation and what it would involve; ask yourself, friends, and family what the opposite career choice would look like. Sometimes it helps to turns things inside out to get a fresh look at the possibilities.
3. Combine the occupations to make new ones. For example, a chef and a teacher could lead to a career as a curriculum designer for a culinary arts school.
4. Stimulate new career options by observing the environment around you. Label every occupation you come across throughout the day.

Then, using the interests described above, generate new occupational choices.

5. Research books on emerging careers and future career trends. Select occupations with interest themes like yours. Determine the ones that are a good fit for you and write them down.

6. Investigate professional associations and trade magazines associated with the areas you selected for career possibilities. These are places where new occupations in those fields are likely to be discussed.

7. Ponder your work experiences to understand how your interests have impacted your career satisfaction in the past.

Identifying Interests by Studying Past Experiences

Examining your past employment can uncover important insights about future career possibilities. Like most people, you probably think about your work experiences in terms of a title you held, the company you worked for, and the functions of your position. This way of thinking constricts your ability to see all of your strengths and capabilities. Contributions you made are only partially related to the knowledge or specific functions of your jobs. Most of your value emerged as a result of the way you incorporated your values, interests, and personality traits into your work.

Let's explore beyond the titles and position descriptions for two nurses in the same hospital. Both are good nurses and consistently perform all the job functions listed on the position descriptions.

One is a good nurse because he is warm and friendly. He asks about family and friends and makes his patients laugh and feel loved. He came up with the idea to have an annual recognition party for nurses. He volunteers his time to plan the event every year. He also created a game for patients that incorporates patient success stories and feel-good rewards. He develops great relationships with support staff so that when he gets behind as a result of talking to patients, they assist him in completing intake forms for new patients.

The other person is a good nurse because she is articulate and thorough in explaining every step of a procedure. She offers details and reasons for every action she takes and manages her patients as carefully and precisely as possible. She is impeccable with her record keeping. She updated reporting procedures over the years to improve efficiency and help others track information more readily. While she is very committed to her patients, she prefers to send apprentices to chat with them instead of conducting these "social" rounds herself.

Both nurses perform the same job, and both make the patients feel good, but for very different reasons. Both contribute to the department and add value, but in different ways. Both prefer different aspects of their jobs and delegate different elements.

You can learn a lot about yourself by examining your past experiences for elements that provide vital pieces of the career identity puzzle. Ask yourself the following questions.

1. How have you made past positions fit you?
2. What extra responsibilities have you assumed in your past jobs that were not part of your job description?
3. What activities do you volunteer to do in your job?
4. What tasks do you avoid doing, delegate, or put off until the last minute?

Likes and Dislikes

List the last three positions you have held. What did you like about each position? What did you dislike? The objective is to focus on exploring careers that have more of your likes than dislikes—in terms of your own activities as well as the work environment. By completing this exercise, you will be better prepared to know what you like and what you want to avoid in your career.

1. Position/Title:_____

Likes	Dislikes
_____	_____
_____	_____
_____	_____
_____	_____

2. Position/Title:_____

Likes	Dislikes
_____	_____
_____	_____
_____	_____
_____	_____

3. Position/Title:_____

Likes	Dislikes
_____	_____
_____	_____
_____	_____
_____	_____

It is important to write down your interests on paper so that you can compare them with your future career options. These interests can also help you to formulate questions for the interview to understand what the company is really like.

Fascinations

You do not choose to be fascinated. Instead, fascinations seem to pursue you. Many people with a fully developed, satisfying career believe that their work or calling found them. They cannot really explain why they are good at their vocation or why it is so rewarding to them. They do know that they find themselves drawn to a certain type of work and that they are energized by it. In exploring career options, it is imperative that you learn to notice what fascinates you.

FASCINATIONS ASSESSMENT

Continue to create your plot by developing a list of your fascinations. As you complete the exercise below, remember that fascinations are not *verbs*; they are *nouns*. You are fascinated not by "repairing" but by motors. You are fascinated not by "traveling" but by foreign cultures.

Fascinations are:

Topics

Issues

School subjects

Hobbies

Industries

Causes

You are fascinated by something when:

• You really listen when the topic/subject is discussed.

• You read magazines or articles about it.

- You are glad when the topic comes up in conversation or on television.

- You remain interested in it year after year.

- You buy or read books about the subject.

Your fascinations include:

Examples: professionals, human development, change, approaches to learning, innovation

1.

2.

3.

4.

5.

6.

7.

8.

9.

10.

Combining Fascinations

Now that you know some of your primary fascinations, you can stimulate your own creative thinking and brainstorming to generate ideas about new career options. Take the fascinations listed above and combine them in order to generate even more fascinations. Many inventions

"Vision is the art of seeing the invisible."

—*Jonathan Swift*

and breakthroughs are the result of combining two seemingly divergent things to create something new. For example, when the ancients mixed soft copper and even softer tin, the result was hard bronze. Also, when Johannes Gutenberg combined the wine press and the coin punch, he invented movable type and the printing press.

List your combinations below.

Example: professionals + change = performance evaluations

1.

2.

3.

4.

5.

Associating Fascinations

Another way to stimulate your understanding of fascinations is by association. Much of your thinking is associative: one idea or concept triggers another. Take one of your fascinations and generate a series of word associations. For example, the word "work" might trigger the following associations:

work—play—actor—star—sun—light—bulb—tulips—kiss—love—tennis—net—profit—prophet—oracle—auricle—heart—life

Select five fascinations from above and write them in the space provided below. Take each one and a series of word associations until you have made an association cluster of at least 10 words. This activity stimulates thinking in creative ways and will help bring to light new ideas and thoughts.

Example: performance evaluation—help—growth—leadership—community—advocate—group work—family—relationships—emotion—therapist—diagnosis—treatment—wellness

1.

2.

3.

4.

5.

Childhood Fascinations

Fascinations can emerge early in life, and sometimes awareness of them is lost over time. A great way to rediscover your fascinations is to find a picture of yourself or photo album from between the ages of 6 and 10. Use the pictures to remember what you were like as a child. These years mark an important stage in life when you were old enough to have unique interests and fascinations but still too young to be caught up in cultural expectations. You can learn a lot about yourself by remembering your childhood. Your childhood is the time when clues and insights about your authentic self are waiting to be discovered.

Look at the picture(s) and remember.

- What did you like to do at recess?

- Who were your friends?

- What games did you play?

- What outfits/clothes did you like to wear?

- What shows did you watch?

- What was your favorite story/children's book?

- What were your favorite food, color, animal, and song?

- Who was your favorite hero/heroine?

Remember your bedroom.

- What did it look like?

Remember your birthdays.

- What toys or gifts did you get?

Continued exploration of your interests and fascinations can be a lot of fun and will assist you in tapping into insights about yourself that you have not thought about in a while.

Finding Yourself Center Stage—Completion of Act One

Each of the assessments and exercises leading up to Act Two are not meant to be used alone; they need to be used in concert with one another. No assessment can tell you who you are or what you should do; they simply serve as a vehicle for encouraging exploration and developing clarity and direction.

Remember, the process of finding yourself center stage is not about obtaining a title; no one title encompasses all of who you are. You will discover a variety of options to pursue, but it is important to understand that they will be directed by you, not someone else. Happiness is about doing what you want to do, not conforming to someone else's expectations.

As you prepare to transform all the information you collected in the first three chapters into a marketing campaign and strategic action plan, be sure to keep your focus on what you've learned during the career exploration, not your past experiences. Your past experiences simply provide relevant information that supports what you want in your future; the rest is history, literally.

In chapter 4, The Script, you will transform the insights you have learned about yourself into a professional résumé, which is the document that communicates your value to employers. Your talents, gifts, and strengths should be easily identifiable in your new résumé. Even if your past jobs have been just that—jobs—not careers that held passion and excitement, you still made that position fit your personal style. Make sure that what you liked most about your work experiences is described in accomplishment statements and highlighted. The development of your résumé and cover letter needs to reflect the wonderful gems you have identified about yourself in the first half of this book. What you have written in these pages so far should serve as the template for writing your résumé and cover letter.

You cannot turn your work into play if you do not represent yourself at center stage. Too frequently, the essential information brought to light in the career-counseling portion of a program is left on the pages of the assessment results and never transferred to the documents that are meant to help you secure a more meaningful career.

ACT TWO

Career Search
Implementation—
Turning Your Work
into Play

The Script

BY THE CLOSE of Act One, my objective was to have brought each reader to a place where it is now possible for you to capture and more fully embrace the entire scope and range of your unique constellation of talents and abilities. Having now readied yourself in terms of both content and outlook, you are prepared to write your personal script for the play of your life.

> *"Choose a job you love, and you will never have to work a day in your life."*
>
> —Confucius

The information you've collected so far will serve as your template in tackling the next tasks: writing your résumé and cover letter. The conventional résumé merely reports what you have done and where you have been. These outdated résumés focus strictly on the past, not your future. It is absolutely essential that you do more with your résumé. More important, your résumé must showcase your unique strengths and talents so that it conveys to any potential employer the full value of what you can contribute to their organization.

After creating a résumé and cover letter that are true to who you really are and describe all the value you bring employers, you will begin to bring these exciting new marketing tools to life. This portion of the book is your Production. In the production phase of the play of your life, you will learn about the best way to build a presence for yourself in the marketplace. Many people think this is accomplished by getting their résumés out on the Internet or sending them en masse to employers, hoping one will respond with an offer. The production takes a very different approach—a strategic approach that ensures your time is spent wisely and your activities are meaningful and fruitful. The active search portion of the play of your life is a lot of work, and you will be asked to rethink how you have engaged searches in the past. While it is a production, it is extremely worthwhile and necessary to achieving your own personal stardom.

Act Two does not stop at helping you get your foot in the door through networking and strategic planning. One chapter is dedicated to making certain that you excel in the interview and do indeed get offered the position. And other chapters complete the play of your life with valuable skills development on writing thank-you letters, preparing references, and negotiating offers.

You have done it—accumulated all the important information about yourself to begin writing the script for the play of your life. Now, as they say in the biz, the show must go on! Here is how to turn your work into your play. . . .

Having a clear understanding of yourself is essential, especially during those rough patches in career transition when you are more likely to focus entirely on the past in presenting yourself to network contacts and potential employers. The reason the play of your life starts out with an exploration that results in your articulating a strong awareness of your most satisfying qualities and characteristics is that it affords you a true and constant beacon that will always light your way to your future success, even when times are rough and you feel the most insecure.

The résumé you write will serve as the culmination of all the hard work you completed in the previous chapters. In this section, you will combine all the elements that influence your career satisfaction into a unified picture. Just as a play follows a script, your résumé should synthesize the information you have gathered about yourself and make it a resource that communicates your value to employers. Your résumé is a powerful articulation of the career you want for yourself. Also in this section, you will learn to write cover letters that communicate how the career you want for yourself is important to the prospective employer. Having a great résumé that describes your value is one piece, but making sure the employer knows how to incorporate your value into the company is equally important.

You probably have previous versions of your résumés on file, but before you revise them, please review this chapter. Instead of teaching you how to once again update your standard résumé, this chapter asks you to throw out your old ideas about what the function and purpose of a résumé truly is. By helping you gain a whole perspective on developing a résumé, I will introduce you to a new approach to marketing yourself in the workplace. While a résumé is rarely, if ever, sufficient to land you the job, it often determines whether you get a shot at it. Like a theatre ticket, your résumé is what gets you in the door.

Your résumé needs to describe the future value you offer an employer. But when your career path is altered, by choice or not, it can throw off your confidence. Leaving a position can bring about feelings of frustration, anger, loss, and depression. When struggling with loss of a position, it is common to feel a sense of futility. This futility turns your attention to the past. These feelings can impact how you perceive and express the value you offer an employer and negatively affect how you write your résumé.

By recognizing your vulnerability to self-doubt during this time, you can avoid falling into a trap of negativity. It is important to begin repositioning your thinking toward future opportunities.

Like many people, you probably use outdated thinking to understand your current position. What I mean by this is that most people entered the workforce during a time when it was appropriate to believe that the company managed your career. The company put forth the "corporate ladder" and described the milestones you must reach in order to climb it. You did not have to personally manage your career; it was taken care of by the company. Companies liked it this way because it helped ensure that you did not leave.

Corporations want you to think company first, position second, industry third, unique skills and talents last. Notice that when you ask people what they do for a living, they will almost always associate with the company first. "I work for AT&T." "I am an IBMer." "I am a state employee." "I work for Coca-Cola." Companies spend enormous amounts of money giving you items to wear and brand you as a company person. This is a great strategy because if you associate more with the company than you do with your profession, you will be less likely to leave that company even when an attractive offer from another employer is put in front of you.

This made great sense for employees to buy into when they were offered job security and were considered an integral part of the corporate fabric. But now the willingness to align yourself with the company over and above your individual talents and strengths is extremely risky. I frequently hear people say, "I lost my job." In reality, they did not lose anything. Their jobs were taken from them and moved offshore or completely eliminated. These people feel like they have less. If you lose something, you have less than before. Without knowing it, millions of people are being their own worst enemy by letting themselves think about their career in antiquated terms. If companies are no longer loyal to you, then why are you loyal to them? Be aware of how you describe yourself in relation to your career. You are more than a company employee, and when a company takes a position away, you still possess all the talents, experiences, and accomplishments the next day. You are simply no longer applying them in that particular company. The values, personality preferences, strengths, talents, interests, and fascinations you assessed in the first half of the book are what you bring to a future employer.

If you have not established a clear career direction, you are likely to focus entirely on where you have been when you present yourself to network contacts and employers. *The Play of Your Life* purposely started with an exploration of your internal career description so that you could develop clarity and direction for your future.

The exercises in the first three chapters were designed to help you find yourself center stage. They serve as your guide to articulating in your résumé who you are and what you do. Traditional résumés are focused on the past, not your future. It is absolutely essential that you recognize your talents and that you have enormous value to contribute to an organization. Once you can embrace your strengths and feel excited about your accomplishments, you are ready to begin building a powerful résumé.

Your Audience as the Guide for Developing Your Résumé

As you begin to develop your résumé, ask yourself the following essential questions.

- Who are my ideal employers?

- What do they value?

- What motivates them?

- What skills and experiences do they value?

- What roles are critical within the organization?

The answers to these questions reinforce your orientation toward the future and provide you with a clear image of your consumers and what they value.

Consider an example of advertisements used by pharmaceutical companies. They all concentrate on how great you will feel after using their products. The products are never mentioned or talked about. For allergy medication, the commercial is a scene of people rolling in fields of flowers with big smiles. These companies are selling solutions, not drugs. And it works fabulously.

A company with a successful focus on the consumer is Coca-Cola. Coca-Cola sells carbonated syrup, but commercials never describe the company as a manufacturer of carbonated syrup. Commercials show beautiful models and happy people who want to "teach the world to sing in perfect harmony." Coke sells satisfaction, not soda. Cingular Wireless, Volkswagen, Budweiser, and L'Oréal are all successful at marketing to the consumer without directly marketing the product itself.

Marketing is more about the consumer, your prospective employer, than about you. Begin paying attention to how companies market their products, and you will observe this valuable lesson that clearly applies to your successful résumé development. As you begin to develop your résumé, focus only on your positive qualities that relate to prospective employers.

Good Résumé versus Great Résumé

There are clear differences between a good résumé and a great résumé.

- A good résumé is a glorified application. This type of résumé explains to the hiring manager the following information in this order: dates of employment, companies, ti-

> *"Tell me what company you keep, and I'll tell you who you are."*
>
> —*Anonymous*

tles held, and job functions. It concludes with when and where you received your education. It is good because the hiring manager can get a clear summation of your past experience and education.

- A great résumé is a marketing brochure. This résumé highlights the scope and depth of your experience. It describes the expertise you have developed throughout your career that relates to your future employer's needs. A great résumé communicates a compelling reason for the prospective employer to need and want *your* services.

Good résumés identify where you went to school, the jobs you have had, and your responsibility in those jobs. Great résumés extract the relevant accomplishments from your past experiences and highlight them. This prompts the interviewer to ask about them with the future in mind.

Great résumés also pave the way for great interviews. A well-crafted résumé will prompt the interviewer to target specific areas that are most relevant to the open position. A résumé that lists everything you have ever done requires you to be prepared to talk about all these things in an interview. It is difficult to prepare for such an extensive interview and can lead the interview astray.

Create a Great Résumé

Once you have adopted a future-focused orientation, you are ready to create your résumé. The presentation of your information, the layout, and the language you use to communicate value are extremely important. There are only two things you can be sure a hiring manager will do when reviewing your résumé: (1) Hiring managers will begin reviewing a résumé by starting at the top, and they will read the lines from left to right. (2) Their first impression will have the greatest impact and will influence how they perceive you. It creates the lens through which all other information is filtered.

Based on these principles, it is essential that the most relevant, important information be presented at the top and along the left side of your résumé. The least important information should be at the bottom and along the right side.

Résumé Format

In order to transform your résumé from a good résumé to a great résumé, concentrate on using your layout and language most effectively. Here's how.

HEADINGS

The main heading is where you provide contact information for the hiring managers. Your main heading lets them know who you are and where you can be reached. This section should be designed like a professional letterhead. Résumés are formal documents, so you should not use abbreviations here.

Example:

FRAN C. SMITH

1153 Terry Avenue • Atlanta, Georgia 30306 • francsmith@aol.com • 404-555-1234

The main heading highlights your name and provides the contact information on one line, followed by a divider line. This format saves space that can be dedicated to communicating more of your strengths. Notice that it is not necessary to label the phone number or e-mail address; these items are understood. Be as concise as possible.

Use the same heading on your references page, cover letters, and thank-you letters. By creating a professional-looking letterhead, you offer a consistent image to the hiring manager. It also allows the hiring manager to quickly access your contact information on every document.

Section headings are titles you assign to different areas of your résumé.

For example, your employment section will have one heading. Your education and community activities sections will have their own headings.

Section headings are extremely important. A section name influences how the hiring manager perceives the information within the heading. If you use an objective statement as your first section heading, you communicate your needs to the hiring manager. You are saying to the hiring manager, "My objective is to get a job."

If your first section is a summary of qualifications, your section heading communicates the value you offer the hiring manager. You focus the reader on the ways you will meet the company's needs. This heading also tells the hiring manager you are indeed "qualified" for the position. You summarize the qualifications that will be explained in detail in the remainder of the résumé.

A summary of qualifications should be confined to three high-impact statements.

- The first statement should highlight your years of experience in the profession and industry.

- The second statement should identify the areas of expertise you want to emphasize.

- The third statement should identify personal attributes that are important to the role and company.

Example:

SUMMARY OF QUALIFICATIONS

Offers more than 10 years of progressive advancement in the manufacturing industry, serving as an operations executive. Demonstrates a proven record of success in leading as many as 250 associates, streamlining business processes, and managing multiple projects delivered on time and within budget. Possesses exceptional communication skills and the ability to develop high-performance teams.

While "Summary of Qualifications" is the best section heading to begin your résumé, there are several exceptions to the rule. If you fall into one of these exceptions, then you need to consider beginning your résumé with an objective statement.

Exception 1: Clarity. If you are making a transition by applying for a position that diverges from your past experience, an objective statement is needed, since your skills are not an obvious or solid match for the position. Use the objective statement to clarify your interest in the position and show that your skills are transferable.

Exception 2: Intent. If you do not use a cover letter to introduce your purpose in sending the résumé, an objective statement is appropriate. The objective statement communicates the purpose of your résumé. In this circumstance, the objective should be very direct and specific to the prospective company and position.

Additional section headings that are useful in constructing a résumé that communicates value to a hiring manager include:

- Areas of Expertise
- Career Highlights
- Professional Achievements
- Key Accomplishments

These sections follow your summary of qualifications. They emphasize specific strengths you have developed throughout your career. These sections provide an opportunity to bring special attention to experiences that are most relevant to the hiring manager, regardless of when and where they occurred.

For example, if you want to convey that your experience as a leader is a key asset even though your leadership experience has been in a different industry, you can emphasize this in a leadership experience section. This way, the hiring manager focuses on your leadership qualifications first before reading about it later in the context of the industry.

Be careful not to give too much information in this section. For example, if you create an areas of expertise section, ideally confine your expertise to four areas and not more than six areas. Listing too many areas dilutes the depth of expertise. The same holds true for accomplishments and achievements. Focus the hiring manager's attention on your most important accomplishments by creating three strong statements.

Select a high-impact section heading for your employment section. Do not use "Employment History" or "Work Experience." These headings are vague and generic. The terms *employment* and *work* define virtually every type of job available, from soda jerk or paperboy to corporate CEO or marketing director.

Instead, create a compelling section heading that optimizes your experience. The following section headings are appropriate for professional résumés. They communicate a career path, versus a series of jobs.

- Career Progression

- Career Advancement

- Professional Experience

Now you are ready to arrange the most important information at the top left of the page and least important information at the bottom right. Start with what is most compelling to the hiring manager. Begin with your professional title or your industry and company name. Then list the location and your dates of employment to the right.

Example:

MARKETING DIRECTOR
XYZ Industries, Atlanta, Georgia   *June 1992–June 2002*

Résumé Length

There are differing opinions regarding the appropriate length of a résumé. The general rule regarding résumé length is:

- One page for less than 10 years of professional experience
- Two pages for more than 10 years of professional experience

However, this rule can vary depending on your circumstances. For example, say you have more than 20 years of professional experience. If the last 5 to 10 years are the most relevant and substantial, then a one-page résumé that highlights this experience may be more appropriate.

This conversation between an author and his editor illustrates why you should pay attention to your résumé length.

EDITOR: I like your book except for the ending.

AUTHOR: What's wrong with the ending?

EDITOR: It should be closer to the beginning.

More is not better in résumé writing. Your objective is to keep the hiring manager's attention focused on your skills that add immediate value to the company. If you describe every experience and function of your entire career, you risk diverting the focus away from the parts of your résumé that are most important.

Additionally, if you put every single experience on your résumé, you have to be prepared to discuss every single experience in the interview. As a result, your interview will be more difficult to prepare for and you run the risk of being asked about experiences that are not relevant to the position. You may be perceived as "not a good fit" because, based on your résumé, the hiring manager asked about the wrong skill, rather than what was needed for that particular position.

Résumé Content

Transform your résumé from a description of job functions to a series of accomplishment statements that are of interest to the hiring manager. To do this, read your job function statements and ask yourself:

- What was the purpose of this responsibility/project/task?

- How was this job function relevant to the company?

- Did this job function save time, save money, increase revenue, improve a process/policy/infrastructure?

The answers to these questions are typically the most important elements of the résumé to the hiring manager and need to be communicated clearly.

CREATE ACCOMPLISHMENT STATEMENTS

Writing accomplishment statements is a simple three-step process.

1. Start with an action verb to attract the hiring manager's attention.
2. Next, provide concise information about the task, project, problem.
3. Then describe the result in terms of money made or saved, percent increased/decreased, time frame, or quantity.

Examples:

- Developed an optimal merchandising process focusing on retailer profitability, resulting in a 53 percent increase in sales and a 15 percent profit increase.

- Designed the Fundamental Equity investment product, which outperformed the S&P 500 by 15 percent.

- Implemented 401(k) programs that increased employee participation to 93 percent and contributed to higher employee productivity.

- Created a profit-and-loss statement by product, which resulted in eliminating 20 percent of the product line that was found to be unprofitable.

- Penetrated new business arenas, using a joint-venture direct-marketing approach, which generated over $60 million in new sales.

CREATE RECOGNITION STATEMENTS

Another method for articulating the value you bring to hiring managers is to leverage experiences that were recognized by employers, organizations, or others. Recognition statements help to show the employer that others see value in your work and recognize you as valuable. The saying "There is comfort in numbers" applies here. If hiring managers believe you have been important to others, they will probably infer that you can serve an important role for them. One way to demonstrate that others found you to be an important contributor is to integrate the following verbs into your descriptions.

- Promoted to . . .

- Recruited to . . .

- Chosen by . . . to . . .

- Selected to . . .

- Recognized for . . .

- Awarded for excellence in . . .

ADD SUBSTANCE

Review the language of your job function statements. Make sure that every statement describes a strength or variation of the same strength. Take the example of a manager:

Before . . .	After . . .
MANAGER, Company, location, date	MANAGER, Company, location, date
Managed . . .	Promoted within xx months
Managed . . .	Directed . . .
Managed . . .	Oversaw . . .
Managed . . .	Pioneered . . .
Managed . . .	Led . . .
Managed . . .	Initiated . . .
Managed . . .	Supervised . . .
Managed . . .	Launched . . .
Managed . . .	Spearheaded . . .

What you did has not changed, but by differentiating your language, you give greater depth, breadth, and scope to your experience. Résumés do not read like books. They are made up of a series of concise, powerful statements that emphasize your skills. Eliminate use of pronouns like *I, our, we,* and *my.* It is understood that what is on your résumé is about you.

CREATE SELLING STATEMENTS

After completing your accomplishment statements, read them out loud to listen for whether they are "telling" a hiring manager what you have done or "selling" your accomplishments. Selling your accomplishments allows hiring managers to envision what you will do for them in the future. You are not just saying what you did; you are saying you did it well.

Example: Instead of saying what you have done, add "selling" phrases, such as the ones listed below, to the beginning of your statements.

- Successfully . . .

- Demonstrated expertise . . .

- Met the challenge to . . .

- Established a proven record of success . . .

- Consistently achieved corporate goals by . . .

Remember, a good résumé tells the hiring manager what you have done, but a great résumé sells your accomplishments.

CUSTOMIZE YOUR RÉSUMÉ

Different words elicit different concepts and images. If an architect looks at an opening between two rooms and thinks "door," that is what will be designed. But if the architect thinks "passageway," something very different, like a hallway, archway, tunnel, or courtyard, may be designed. Various descriptions can lead a reader's thinking in different directions. This is the rationale for customizing a résumé.

You may want to customize your résumé to make it specific to a particular profession or industry. A good way to do this is to identify keywords or functions that are familiar to your prospective profession or industry. You can collect this information by reviewing job descriptions, industry literature, and professional trade magazines and Web sites. Use this information as a cross-reference when creating your résumé. Try to incorporate as many keywords as possible.

Conversely, review your résumé for terminology that is not consistent with your targeted industry or profession. If your language is specific to a different field, generalize the terminology so that the hiring manager will more easily understand it. Review your résumé for any language that is not known to the general reader and rewrite it so it is relevant.

Make sure your words are relevant to the hiring manager. Do not discuss a specific technology that was proprietary to a company and is not known outside the company. Replace the name of that specific technology with "proprietary software," "software," or "technology." Choose words broad enough for the reader to understand.

For example, assume your role required you to use RADAR, LEGACY 4000, and XMAR systems for tracking insurance claims. Instead of saying something so specific to the industry that only people in your company or industry would know what you are talking about, say, "Used multiple proprietary software programs to manage critical client information." This allows prospective employers to realize you that you are a technically competent person. When you keep the actual names of the software programs on your résumé, you run the risk of having prospective employers dismiss it as inconsequential information simply because they do not know those specific tools.

CLARIFY RÉSUMÉ STATEMENTS

Lastly, examine your résumé for bland or generic terms like *worked with, did things.* Add high-impact terms, such as *partnered with* and *collaborated with.* Also, if you use the word *things*, replace it with a description of the specific projects you did.

Résumé Content Exercises

ACCOMPLISHMENT STATEMENT EXERCISE

Statements that powerfully communicate accomplishments are provided below. Select the statements that apply to you and incorporate them into your résumé.

- Increased sales or profits

- Improved quality

- Reduced costs

- Improved customer service

- Designed a procedure

- Wrote a procedures manual

- Stimulated productivity

- Implemented a marketing plan

- Developed a budget

- Taught a course

- Coordinated a relocation

- Penetrated a new market

- Supervised staff

- Developed a team

- Facilitated change

- Researched and analyzed trends

- Reorganized a system

- Initiated a technical breakthrough

- Streamlined a process

- Presented an innovation

- Negotiated contracts

- Recruited professionals

- Developed a training program

- Designed new products

All of these are examples of how you:

1. Made money for the company
2. Saved money for the company
3. Made processes easier for the company
4. Saved time for the company
5. Improved productivity or efficiency

Using the statements and accomplishments above, create 10 accomplishment statements.

1. Action Verb:

   Project/Event:

   Result:

   _____

2. Action Verb:

   Project/Event:

   Result:

   _____

3. Action Verb:

   Project/Event:

   Result:

   _____

4. Action Verb:

   Project/Event:

   Result:

---

5. Action Verb:

   Project/Event:

   Result:

---

6. Action Verb:

   Project/Event:

   Result:

---

7. Action Verb:

   Project/Event:

   Result:

---

8. Action Verb:

   Project/Event:

   Result:

   _____

9. Action Verb:

   Project/Event:

   Result:

   _____

10. Action Verb:

    Project/Event:

    Result:

    _____

SELLING STATEMENT EXERCISE

After completing your accomplishment statements, review the list of high-impact phrases below. This list describes you, your personality, your leadership style, and your ability to effect organizational change and improvement. Select keywords and phrases and use them to enhance your accomplishment statements.

- Accelerated career track

- Aggressive turnaround leadership

- Benchmarking

- Best in class

- Business process redesign

- Capturing cost reductions

- Catalyst for change

- Change agent

- Change management

- Competitive market positioning

- Creative business leader/problem solver

- Cross-functional expertise

- Decisive management style

- Deliver strong and sustainable gains

- Distinguished performance

- Driving customer loyalty initiatives

- Driving innovation

- Emerging business ventures

- Entrepreneurial drive/vision

- Executive leadership

- Fast-track promotion

- High-impact/-caliber/-performance

- Innovative leader

- Multidiscipline industry expertise

- Organizational leader

- Outperforming market competition

- Peak performer

- Performance improvement

- Pioneering technologies

- Proactive leader/manager

- Productivity improvement

- Start-up and high-growth organization

- Strategic and tactical operations

- Strong and sustainable gains/growth

- Team building/team leadership

- Technologically advanced

- Visionary leader

- World-class leadership

- World-class organization

THE IDEAL-JOB-DESCRIPTION EXERCISE

When you have completed the first draft of your résumé, place your hand over the main heading at the top and read the résumé as if you were reading a job description. Ask yourself, "Does this sound like something I want to do, and is it important to the profession/industry I am targeting?" The ideal-job-description exercise is important because the résumé must describe what you want to do. If it does not, you will end up getting hired to perform a role that is not in alignment with your internal career description.

THE FRIEND EXERCISE

Distribute your résumé to close friends, family, and references. Ask them, "Does this résumé communicate my strengths and experiences in a manner that is compelling to a hiring manager in this industry/profession?" The friend test is important because a résumé that highlights your accomplishments and the expertise you offer is difficult to develop. Your strengths may be hard for you to see because they come so naturally to you; they may not be clearly articulated. Friends and family can be excellent resources for pointing out strengths that you have not recognized as important.

THE PSEUDO-EMPLOYER EXERCISE

Have the people you used in the friend exercise give your résumé to someone who does not know you. Have them answer the following questions: "For what type of position is this person well-suited?" "What profession?" "What industry?" "What are this person's greatest strengths?" "What kind of compensation should this person expect?"

The pseudo-employer exercise is the best indicator of how a prospective employer who has never met you will react to the résumé. Both you and the people who know you are unconsciously influenced by the knowledge of your strengths and capabilities. This creates a blind spot to aspects of your résumé that need clarification or development.

If your résumé passes these three exercises, then congratulations! Your résumé is ready to go to market. This is your marketing brochure, and you must be comfortable with it. If you receive conflicting feedback from different sources, remember that with résumés, as with most things in life, everyone has an opinion. Finalize your résumé based on the feedback you feel is worthwhile to produce a great marketing piece.

The following sections include a résumé checklist for your résumé critique. Additionally, there are several résumé examples that illustrate the concepts discussed above.

Résumé Checklist

Make sure your résumé meets the following criteria. Go through this checklist each time you change your résumé.

1. Visual impact
   - ☐ Professional-looking document
   - ☐ Quality résumé paper
   - ☐ Easy to scan

2. Layout
   - ☐ Visually appealing
   - ☐ Easy to read
   - ☐ Good margins and use of white space
   - ☐ Good use of highlighting (that is, bold, underline, italics)

3. Length
   - ☐ Could the résumé tell the same story if it were shorter?

4. Writing style
   - ☐ Clear and concise
   - ☐ Logical flow of information
   - ☐ Jargon/abbreviations kept to a minimum
   - ☐ Consistent style and form

5. Action-, achievement-, and results-oriented
   - ☐ Use of action verbs
   - ☐ Results: increase in productivity/profit

                       reduction in manpower/cost

                       save time or money

6. Specific and relevant
   - ☐ Résumé supports career objective

7. Complete and accurate
   - ☐ No typographical or spelling errors

8. The bottom line
   - ☐ Does the résumé arouse interest from the employer?
   - ☐ Does the résumé get the applicant invited for an interview?

Résumé Examples

What follows are examples of two different résumé formats. The long-format examples start on the opposite page. These résumés are detailed and incorporate annotations on the listed experiences. The one-page examples start on page 132. Because of the format of this book, the one-page résumés fill two pages. However, the content of these résumés actually fits on a single, standard 8½-by-11-inch page.

Long-Format Examples

NAME

123 Smith Street • Sunshine, New York 10001 • 718-335-1234 • name@yahoo.com

Senior Executive Profile

President / CEO / Division Vice President
Start-Up Ventures / Turnarounds / High-Growth Companies /
Fortune 100 Companies
Wholesale Distribution / U.S. and International Markets

Twenty-year senior management career. Expertise in building, revitalizing, and optimizing organizational infrastructure, products, technologies, processes, measurement systems, and sales marketing strategies to produce high-performance results.

PROFESSIONAL HIGHLIGHTS

• Spearheaded strategic business development efforts that increased sales from $110 million to $300 million while directing $41 million in inventory and covering a sales territory in 13 states.

• Produced a 25% increase in wholesale profits and an 11% increase in retail profits for a $100 million wholesale distributor and 25 retail stores.

• Successfully directed a corporate relocation to London involving a company transition from a 50,000-square-foot facility into a state-of-the-art 80,000-square-foot facility. Oversaw development of the infrastructure for all shipping and receiving processes and procedures.

CAREER PROGRESSION

SENIOR CONSULTANT

Bryant Partners International   *New York, New York 2000–Present*

Report directly to chief officers of multiple distributors, offering advice and counsel in all aspects of business growth and development. Notable clients include Nile Rodgers' Sumthing Distribution, Mötley Crüe's Beyond Records, and Evander Holyfield's RealDeal Records.

• Spearheaded direct sales programs for distribution companies.

• Collaborated with Rodgers and Hammerstein during the creation of a joint venture to create a record label company.

- Initiated and implemented sales and new business development plans that assisted companies in increasing revenues while maintaining expenses.

PRESIDENT

Platinum Entertainment/PED Corporation   *Atlanta, Georgia 1999–2000*

Recruited by former Time Warner executives to oversee operations of a wholesale music distributor and record labels spanning the United States, Europe, Canada, and Asia. Challenged to improve company position through strategic enhancements in sales, marketing, operations, warehouse, and the art department as well as studios. Served as key leader to major clients throughout the world.

- Initiated, developed, and executed plans for a new infrastructure to align processes and procedures within warehouse shipping, receiving, and inventory.

- Orchestrated an international move to London that repositioned the company to better meet the needs of European clients.

- Improved sales performance through effective leadership and organizational development program built on teamwork, incentive programs, and strategic market analysis.

- Led teams in the development of multiple distribution affiliations in both the United States and Europe, which more than tripled the number of labels distributed throughout the world.

PRESIDENT

Pacific Coast One-Stop   *Simi Valley, California 1997–1999*

Oversaw all operations for $100 million wholesale music and video distributor and 25 music retail stores. Responsible for opening new retail stores, bringing in major retail chain business to wholesale area, setting sales quotas, and creating yearly budget.

- Successfully drove wholesale profits up 25% in less than 18 months through increased interaction with customers, co-managers, and employees.

- Reduced expenses by 30% through aggressive analysis of business operations, reducing staff, and ensuring accountability and production measures were in place.

- Produced aggressive and detailed sales plans and reporting systems to track progress and goal attainment. Presented in-depth presentations to board, resulting in dramatic change.

- Facilitated the negotiation and sale of 15 retail stores, streamlined business operations, and created an 11% increase in retail profits from a previous loss.

- Implemented a strong management-training program focused on profitability and pricing management, resulting in improved profit margins within 18 months.

VICE PRESIDENT

Warner Elektra Atlantic Corporation/
Division of Time Warner   *Los Angeles, California   1980–1997*

Fast-track advancement in multiple sales positions to direct all operations for entertainment industry distribution center. Led senior management team responsible for $41 million in inventory and a sales territory covering 13 states. Responsible for operations in Seattle and San Francisco, including oversight of over 200 employees, marketing, and promotions.

- Achieved "Branch of the Year" multiple times as a result of ability to outperform all other regions in sales, marketing, and operations of a large distribution center.

- Successfully increased sales from $110 million to over $300 million while leading the management team through enormous growth and expansion.

EDUCATION

Bachelor of Science, Business Administration

University of Baltimore—Baltimore, Maryland

PHILANTHROPIC / PROFESSIONAL ASSOCIATION LEADERSHIP

- Scholarship Board—National Association of Recording Merchandisers
- Advisory Board—The Northridge Hospital Foundation
- Advisory Board—Habitat for Humanity

NAME

789 Broad Street • Houston, Texas 77052 • 713-440-6789 • name@earthlink.net

....

Health Care Supply Chain / Sales and Marketing Executive

SUMMARY OF QUALIFICATIONS

Seasoned professional with Fortune 100 company experience in targeting sales with CEOs, CFOs, and COOs; over 18 years' proven ability in sales management and supply chain management, including budgeting and P&L responsibility; possessing leadership ability in the health-care services industry; highly effective in team selling and consensus building; results-oriented in exceeding operational and budgetary goals.

Marquee Healthcare   *Houston, Texas*

REGIONAL SALES MANAGER   *2000–Present*

Marquee Healthcare, a Fortune 100 company, provides on-site management solutions for health care in pharmacy and materials management, including outsourcing, interim management, and consulting services.

Notable Achievements Include:
- Sold consulting and outsourcing services to hospital CEOs, CFOs, and executives throughout the Midwest. Conducted on-site operational needs assessment surveys with potential clients and developed operational goals. Prepared client proposals and needs assessment compilation with financial impact reports.

Result: Developed multiyear contracts in excess of $1 million in revenues with potential savings opportunities in excess of $10 million with major integrated health networks.

- Collaborated with executives of Marquee's business units, Allegiance, Pyxis, and Marquee Consulting.

Result: Designed a comprehensive supply chain solution for large health-care systems and integrated networks.

- Increased penetration of Supplyline (Marquee's product classification and pricing database).

Result: Mayo, Henry Ford Health System, Nebraska Health, University of Missouri Health System, University Hospitals Health System, Cleveland Clinic, and Trinity Health System identified millions in potential savings opportunities.

AMERINET CENTRAL   *Columbus, Ohio*

SENIOR DIRECTOR, ASSISTANT DIRECTOR,   *1989–2000*
AND REGIONAL MANAGER

AmeriNet Central is a primary shareholder of AmeriNet, one of the top three national group purchasing organizations in the country. AmeriNet provides national contracting for over 14,000 health-care members from coast to coast and represents more than $4.9 billion in annual membership purchases.

Notable Achievements Include:

- Developed a regional territory into the second-largest region in the corporation as regional manager.

Result: Sales Achievement and Contract Utilization Awards in 1991, 1992, and 1998. Annual sales increased from $25 million to $230 million, and profitability exceeded budget consistently by better than 100%.

- Successfully directed the sales and marketing of 13 regional territories.

Result: Credited with developing and implementing successful marketing plans for major contract promotions. Instrumental in signing three major affiliates that doubled sales and revenues within 3 years.

- Planned and managed annual trade shows, educational conferences, and group meetings for clients and vendors

Result: Increased attendance resulted in significant increases in utilization of contracts and programs and the overall success in sales and growth in membership.

- Developed the relationship and managed a 2,000-bed integrated delivery network.

Result: Increased revenues by $1.4 million annually and successfully redesigned the agreement for an additional 5-year renewal. Recognized by key clients and senior management for excellence in consultative cost reduction results.

UNITED SHARED SERVICES   *Buffalo, New York*

REGIONAL MANAGER   *1988–1989*

United Shared Services is a regionally based subsidiary of the Western New York Hospital Association whose primary purpose was to provide shared services and group purchasing to acute and non-acute care members throughout western New York.

Notable Achievements Include:

- Credited with increasing contract compliance and utilization of programs.

Result: Increased sales by 200% over a 1-year period, resulting in additional $2.8 million.

- Managed approximately 50 acute and non-acute care accounts.

Result: Increased client satisfaction resulted in increased sales and improved knowledge of cost reduction opportunities, which increased company profitability.

- Facilitated networking opportunities with the Southern Tier Alliance membership.

Result: Recognized by clients and peers as a leader and resource for information.

JAMESTOWN GENERAL HOSPITAL   *Jamestown, New York*
DIRECTOR OF MATERIALS MANAGEMENT   *1982–1988*
AND PURCHASING AGENT

Recruited to Jamestown General Hospital, a New York public community hospital that provided emergency, ICU/CCU, rehabilitation, family practice, and general acute care services in a seven-county community.

Notable Achievements Include:

- Directed and managed a department of 12 FTEs; areas included purchasing, supply distribution, central sterilization, and printing, representing an annual supply budget of $3 million to $4 million and a capital budget of $1 million annually.

Result: Credited with reducing hospital inventories by 45% over a 5-year period. Recognized for exceptional leadership in the development and project management of the hospitalwide telecommunications plan, which included the full replacement of the hospital's telecommunications equipment.

- Established product standards and value analysis committees and processes.

Result: Achieved inventory reductions, improved product utilization and standardization of SKUs, and exceeded savings goals consistently by 25% each year.

EDUCATION

Master of Business Administration
Capital University, Columbus, Ohio

Bachelor of Arts
The Ohio State University, Columbus, Ohio

NAME

456 Jones Street • Pittsburgh, Pennsylvania 15201 • 412-404-4567

....

Senior Executive Profile

President / CEO / Division Vice President
High-Growth Companies / Fortune 500 Companies / Turnarounds
Manufacturing / U.S. and International Markets

Offer 10 years of progressive advancement in senior leadership. Expertise in building, revitalizing, and optimizing organizational infrastructure, products, technologies, processes, measurement systems, and sales marketing strategies to produce high-performance results. Possess MBA from Harvard University.

PROFESSIONAL COMPETENCIES

- Marketing, and business development
- Leadership, training, and development
- Process and productivity improvement
- Performance management
- Product design and development
- Operations and project planning

EXECUTIVE HIGHLIGHTS

- Directed all aspects of the operating activities. Responsible for procurement, product development, and human resources activities of three printing plants. Reported to the chairman and chief executive officer.

- Achieved a 100% increase in revenues from $25 million to $50 million with 50% of the growth among top 10 customers, including Clorox, Coca-Cola, Quaker Oats, Ocean Spray, Procter & Gamble, Tropicana, and Campbell's Soup. Attained in fiscal year 2002 the highest profit margin (5%), return on equity (17%), and asset utilization (1.4 x) of the previous 7 years.

- Led the Executive Steering Committee in developing and introducing the company's vision, strategic growth plan, sales and marketing activities, and continuous improvement initiatives, including Six Sigma implementation.

CAREER PROGRESSION

Tradon Corporation   *Pittsburgh, Pennsylvania   1994–Present*

PRESIDENT, CHIEF OPERATING OFFICER

Promoted from corporate vice president to lead one of the nation's top five full-line consumer goods label manufacturers serving Fortune 500 consumer goods companies. The company's sales revenue is approximately $50 million, with key accounts including Coca-Cola, Clorox, Ocean Spray, Quaker Oats, Pepsi-Cola, and Procter & Gamble. The company operates from three manufacturing facilities located strategically throughout the United States and employs 500 associates. Notable achievements include:

Leadership and Performance Management

- Managed the growth and expansion efforts from two to three state-of-the-art printing plants, resulting in the employment of 250 additional associates. Directed annual budgeted payrolls of over $12 million.

- Achieved greater than 100% throughput gains in two facilities and 50% throughput gains in the third.

- Oversaw the design, engineering, and construction of a $10 million, 66,000-square-foot facility.

- Formulated turnaround of $10 million plant from an annual $2 million loss to a $1 million profit within 1 year.

- Devised and implemented transition to an all-digital pre-press production workflow and color management system requiring a capital investment of more than $1.5 million. Recognized as the first to provide this innovative workflow to Coca-Cola, Ocean Spray, and Welch's.

- Directed the selection and negotiation of over $25 million in annual raw materials and operating supplies.

- Developed and initiated quality and productivity improvements that saved in excess of $4 million annually. Planned and managed Six Sigma rollout, including trainer evaluation and selection, budget of $250,000, project selection, and 4,500 hours of associate training.

- Supervised the information systems department and its annual budget of $150,000.

Product Management

- Directed all product development efforts and an annual departmental budget of $500,000.

- Invented, developed, and introduced patent pending label product lines that attained $14 million of new revenue, with customers including Ocean Spray, Clorox, Welch's, and Procter & Gamble, in its first year.

- Spearheaded the development of five new product lines that generated over 50% of the company's revenue growth; contributed over $15 million in revenues in the next year.

Marketing and Strategic Planning

- Created and presented sales proposals to Fortune 500 customers including Quaker Oats, Clorox, Ocean Spray, Procter & Gamble, Coca-Cola, Gerber Foods, and Campbell's Soup.
- Formulated and implemented strategic account management methodologies to better serve the short- and long-term needs of key customer accounts.
- Broadened strategic account relationships to go beyond the procurement level of key accounts to penetrate engineering, marketing, and operations through solution-selling efforts.
- Evaluated and redirected marketing plan based on a detailed review of the competitive market dynamics of the industry.
- Collaborated on RFP proposals for key accounts amounting to over $150 million in bids.

Kidder, Peabody & Company, Inc.   *New York, New York*   *1992–1993*

FINANCIAL ANALYST—NATURAL RESOURCES
INVESTMENT BANKING GROUP

Kidder, Peabody was a major bulge-bracket full-service investment bank headquartered in New York. Notable achievements include:

- Conducted comprehensive valuation analysis, using common stock comparison and acquisition analyses, for the $1.4 billion stock-for-stock merger of two Fortune 500 minerals companies involved in coal, copper, and gold mining.
- Performed complex spreadsheet analyses used to project pro forma financials, suggest optimal deal structuring, and determine covenant requirements of the $125 million high-yield debt-financed acquisition of a recycled paper mill and paper products company.

EDUCATION AND ADVANCED TRAINING

Harvard University   1995
Master of Business Administration, Recognized with first-year honors

Duke University   1990
Bachelor of Arts in Economics and Business Administration, GPA 3.84/4.00

One-Page Examples

NAME

1257 Lakeshore Drive • Columbus, Ohio 43204 • name@hotmail.com • 614.442.2234

QUALIFICATIONS SUMMARY

Offer over 5 years of leadership experience specializing in personal and professional development. Combine team-building and training skills with proven success offering critical resources to organizations. Report directly to senior management.

CAREER ACCOMPLISHMENTS

TRAINING AND DEVELOPMENT

- Performed new-hire training and follow-up performance evaluations in retail environment
- Conducted weekly counselor training and daily small-group sessions
- Taught youth and adults, using creative teamwork activities, as AmeriCorps volunteer
- Provided mediation training at Capital University
- Elected to Academic Senate by student body and served on committees to improve student life

LEADERSHIP AND SUPERVISION

- Coached sales associates to meet their daily sales goals
- Facilitated urban, rural, and international youth service projects and served as peer counselor
- Directed summer day camp activities for multiple organizations involving diverse populations
- Presented workshops at leadership conferences in 1993 and 1994
- Experienced in volunteer recruitment and coordination within educational institutions

OPERATIONS AND PROJECT MANAGEMENT

- Oversaw logistic services for National Adoption Symposium 2001, including mail-a-thons, volunteer coordination, event registration, and follow-up activities

- Managed advisory board communications for the Dave Thomas Center for Adoption Law
- Organized registrations for professional mediation seminars and provided public relations while reporting directly to the executive director of Capital University Law School

PROFESSIONAL EXPERIENCE

OFFICE MANAGER, *Ashcroft, Fashion Place*   *10/01–Present*

Helped open Delaware branch of the largest family-owned fine jewelry company in the U.S.

ASSOCIATE MANAGER, *Eddie Bauer at Tuttle Crossing*   *6/01–10/01*

High-performance sales coach, key holder and safe access, new-hire orientations

ADMINISTRATOR, *Capital University Law School Centers*   *6/00–7/01*

Dave Thomas National Center for Adoption Law and the Center for Dispute Resolution

CUSTOMER SERVICE REPRESENTATIVE, *Benchmark Outfitters*   *3/99–3/00*

Superior customer service and creative merchandising in specialty retail market

AMERICORPS VOLUNTEER AND
RETREAT TEAM LEADER, *Salesian Missions*   *7/97–8/98*

Led 7,000 students as director of arts program. Organized project in Huatabampo, Mexico

DIRECTOR, *Staff Member CUA Saferides*   *8/93–5/97*

Coordinated student government and campus safety efforts. Included the recruitment, training and scheduling of 30 employees and arranging funding for the program

EDUCATION, ADVANCED TRAINING

Capital University Law School, Columbus, Ohio   8/99–5/00

Catholic University, B.A. Human Resource Management, Washington, D.C.   1998

- *Rev. William Byron Leaders Scholarship* • *Dean's List* •
University Honors Program

NAME

432 Stoneridge Drive • Seattle, Washington 98102 •

206.821.3457 h • 206.234.4879 c • name@earthlink.net

SUMMARY OF QUALIFICATIONS

Over 18 years' experience achieving high growth and strong market presence with 8 years of leadership in an innovative company and 10 years of progressive advancement in financial corporations. Exceptional strategic-planning and problem-solving skills. Charged with measuring productivity and goal attainment. Led teams in achieving national recognition. Managed projects requiring quick turnarounds and extensive troubleshooting. Recognized by peers, customers, and management for consensus building and for creating high-performance teams.

PROFESSIONAL ACCOMPLISHMENTS

ORGANIZATIONAL DEVELOPMENT AND OPERATIONS

- Led the daily operations of a national industrial real estate firm with $97 million in total value in 1994 to over $194 million in 2002. As a key team member, achieved an average 13.7% annual return for 7 consecutive years, resulting in a total 102.8% growth.

- Recognized for empowering regional account managers throughout site acquisition and building as a result of ability to create and analyze each region's impact on the company as a whole.

- Conducted corporate strategy sessions at company board meetings.

STRATEGIC PLANNING AND BUSINESS DEVELOPMENT

- Supported a small, privately owned start-up company from a local presence with 3.2 million square feet in property to a national company with 12.1 million square feet in just 6 years.

- Achieved portfolio upgrades by selling small, obsolete buildings in nonstrategic markets and developing new, state-of-the-art facilities for notable clients, including Hershey, Guess, JVC, Sports Authority, Dell, and Boeing.

- Oversaw regional managers in achieving company growth and pioneering new markets, including California, Florida, South Carolina, Indiana, Tennessee, Texas, Georgia, and Pennsylvania.

CLIENT RELATIONSHIP MANAGEMENT AND TEAM FACILITATION

- Key liaison and mediator between all key constituents, including internal senior management, county officials, industrial tenants, contractors, and vendors. Successfully led teams during new construction and renovations.

- Collaborated with clients from inception through completion of new building process, ensuring projects were completed on time and within strict accordance with permits, architectural plans, and lease specifications.

- Troubleshot wide range of customer issues throughout planning, design, development, and industrial relocations.

CAREER ADVANCEMENT

Bordton Winnsett Properties, Inc.   *1994–2002*

Chosen by CEO to serve in vital leadership roles, including president, corporate manager, and vice president of property management, construction management, and customer service.

SeattleTrust Bank   *1992–1994*

As real estate owned property specialist, sold, managed, and negotiated contracts and lease agreements.

Franklin Federal Savings Association   *1978–1991*

Achieved multiple promotions leading to increased levels of leadership and responsibility, including assistant vice president of commercial credit, assistant property manager, and managing officer of accounts.

EDUCATION

Washington State University, Bachelor of Business Administration

COMMUNITY AND PROFESSIONAL LEADERSHIP

- *Seattle Pet Rescue and Adoption* • *Washington Park Conservancy* •
Friends of Puget Sound

NAME

107 James Street • Charlotte, North Carolina 28204 • 704.899.6367 • name@msn.com

....

SUMMARY OF QUALIFICATIONS

Offer 5+ years' experience and specialized study in alternative dispute resolution (ADR). Experience in ADR systems design, two-party mediation programs, statewide regulatory management of ADR programs, complex, multiparty public disputes. Extensive training in ethical, legal, procedural aspects of the three primary ADR processes: mediation, arbitration, and facilitation, as well as international dispute resolution, negotiation, family law, labor law, employment law, and administrative law. Possess Juris Doctorate, Certificate in Dispute Resolution, and the prestigious Public Service Fellow Certificate with Dean's Special Recognition from The Ohio State University Moritz College of Law.

PROFESSIONAL ADR ACCOMPLISHMENTS

Ohio Commission on Conflict Management, Columbus, Ohio   *January 2002–Present*

Commission does statewide training, consultation, technical assistance in designing ADR programs, facilitation, mediations.

- Researched funding sources and identified grant that doubled commission budget.
- Personally recruited 20 state legislators to attend ADR public dispute seminar.

LEAD Agency, Miami, Oklahoma   *May 2002–Present*

LEAD is EPA's official citizens' group for Tar Creek, which is ranked #1 of 1,200 Superfund sites in the U.S.

- Introduced ADR theories and practices as tools for developing holistic solutions; collaborated with Environmental Protection Agency, Bureau of Indian Affairs, Army Corps of Engineers, and concerned citizens.

Franklin County Court of Common Pleas Juvenile and Domestic Mediation Service   *June 2001–December 2001*

- Conducted and observed mediations; tracked recidivism rates of juvenile defendants who experienced mediation.

Vice President, Moritz College of Law Dispute Resolution Association   *2001–2003*

- Initiated promotional events for Dispute Resolution Certificate candidates; established first annual state-sponsored mediation training for law students and staff.

ADR PUBLICATIONS AND PRESENTATIONS

"Alternative Dispute Resolution and the Tar Creek Superfund Site: Facilitation as a Means toward Holistic Community Recovery from Environmental Disaster," excerpted in *Tar Creek Anthology 2: Our Toxic Place,* ABC Books, 2002.

National Conference on Tar Creek IV: Assessing Damaged Natural Resources, 2002; invited to be presenter.

Careers in Dispute Resolution; presented to students and staff at Grinnell College, 2002.

EDUCATION AND PROFESSIONAL CERTIFICATIONS

The Ohio State University Moritz College of Law,
Columbus, Ohio, Juris Doctorate   May 2003

Certification of Basic Mediation Training,
Franklin County Court of Common Pleas   June 2001

University of Oxford, St. Anne's College, Oxford, England, 2001; European Union law and comparative legal ethics

Grinnell College, Grinnell, Iowa, Bachelor of Arts, English   1999

ADR AND LEGAL CONTRIBUTIONS

Pro Bono Research Group—managing editor for leading-edge organization to provide research for legal aid attorneys

International Competition for Online Arbitration Competition 2003—issued award using UNCITRAL arbitration rules

New York Convention for the Recognition and Enforcement of Foreign Arbitral Awards

Lake County Settlement Week 2000—prepared settlement schedules for 60+ mediations and 40 volunteer mediators

Mediation Board, Grinnell College Office of Community Rights—board member, 1998–1999

Colley Mock Trial, Moritz College of Law—trial participant, 2002

American Mock Trial Association—Championship Flight National Intercollegiate Tournament Competition, 1997

ADDITIONAL EMPLOYMENT EXPERIENCE

Aegis Communications, Joplin, Missouri   *Summer 2000*
Royal Bank of Scotland, Edinburgh, Scotland   *January–May 2000*
Kelley Services, Inc. Minneapolis, Minnesota   *Intermittently 1997–1999*

Assignments: American Express Tax and Business Services, Mergers and Acquisitions; Ecolab, Inc., Food and Beverage Division.

NAME

425 Clarkshead Avenue • Parkersburg, West Virginia 26104 • 304.546.2657 h •

304.567.9235 c • name@iwaynet.net

SUMMARY OF QUALIFICATIONS

Combine Bachelor of Arts from Emory University with over 2 years' experience with PricewaterhouseCoopers, serving as a key resource in the Global Human Resources Solutions business unit. Demonstrate strong record of performance as evidenced by 3.74 GPA and only intern retained by PWC's GHRS group for 3 consecutive years. Offer strong diversity skills, having traveled internationally and studied abroad, in addition to abilities for managing multiple tasks within tight deadlines, communicating well with corporate executives, and utilizing multiple software programs to maximize efficiency in business processes.

PROFESSIONAL EXPERIENCE

PRICEWATERHOUSECOOPERS, LLP
GLOBAL HUMAN RESOURCES SOLUTIONS,
PROFESSIONAL ASSISTANT   *Atlanta, Georgia   May 2001–Present*

- Support unit with over 75 clients and 200 plans in educating and informing clients regarding IRS requirements and terms of legal definitions to ensure accurate data is collected and complies with tax law standards.

- Perform effectively on projects requiring exceptional attention to detail and quick turnaround times. Selected to organize, update, and proofread complex documents, ensuring accuracy and completion of files for notable clients, including the N.Y. Yankees.

- Charged with preparing proposals for prospective clients, including research on many proprietary databases, Internet research, and exhaustive analysis of data, to secure relevant information needed to acquire new business.

- Recognized as point person for questions from new interns and awarded increasing levels of responsibility to the extent of managing client plans from inception through completion.

LEADERSHIP

RESIDENT ADVISOR—*Emory University*   *Atlanta, Georgia   2001–2002*

Chosen to serve a resident advisor for 25 students. Obtained thorough training for emergency response protocols and appropriate actions regarding discipline, dispute resolution, and academic as well as personal challenges confronted by students. Active member of six-person leadership team committed to creating social events for as many as 75 students throughout the school year.

CAMPUS COFFEEHOUSE MANAGER—

Emory University   *Atlanta, Georgia   2001–2002*

Elected by fellow classmates to manage campus coffeehouse. Responsible for two staff, purchasing, inventory, and planning events for customers. Collaborated with university associations and clubs to increase visibility and raise awareness of special events held on campus. Spearheaded the formalization of the coffeehouse by creating structures, policies, and procedures for future management to utilize.

SOCIAL CHAIR—*Dooley's Dolls,*

Emory University   *Atlanta, Georgia   2001–2002*

Partnered with the chapter president to turn around this fledging organization by redefining its role and reputation in the university and launching highly successful community-focused events designed to promote social service in students. Activities included a campuswide toy drive and sock drive for homeless children and adults, creation of over 200 holiday cards for the elderly, and hot chocolate stand fund-raiser for the poor. Received Service Club of the Year Award.

EDUCATION

EMORY UNIVERSITY, Bachelor of Arts, Philosophy and Religion (minor), 2003

4-Year Dean's Scholarship (full-tuition), GPA 3.74, Phi Theta Kappa (Oxford College at Emory University)

UNIVERSITY OF ST. ANDREWS, Study Abroad Program, 2002–2003

Cover Letters

Creating a résumé that truly captures your gifts and talents is a great accomplishment. Your new résumé is a reflection of you and a tool you can be proud to share with others. As you prepare to introduce your qualifications to hiring managers and contacts in your network, you will need to learn how to write cover letters, which frequently accompany résumés.

Cover letters are typically considered less important documents than résumés and, therefore, receive less attention. However, a well-written letter is very important to create a compelling reason for your network to respond to your qualifications. Cover letters are effective when they create a commonality between you and the reader.

The purpose of a résumé is to communicate your accomplishments, experiences, and skills. The purpose of a cover letter is to explain to prospective employers *how* your accomplishments, experiences, and skills add value to the specific needs of the organization or business. This presents an opportunity for the person to respond to something of value rather than feel like he or she is performing a favor for you.

The bottom line is a cover letter gives a compelling reason for the hiring manager to pursue an interview with you.

Content

A cover letter should answer four questions.

1. Why am I a good fit for your organization?
2. How are my qualifications well-matched for a position within your organization?
3. Why is this the right time for me to join your organization?
4. What should be the next step in pursuing an interview?

The answers you provide assist hiring managers in understanding how your résumé fulfills the specific requirements within the organization. A cover letter allows you to draw similarities between your past and the employer's present. This helps them obtain a clearer vision of how you can benefit the organization. A cover letter offers directions that point out how your strengths can be incorporated into the organization.

Employer Focus

A cover letter should be written with a focus on the employer's agenda, not yours.

Think about the way you sort the mail at home. It is likely that the first thing you do is separate the priority mail and junk mail. If the envelope is addressed to "Current Resident," it will likely end up in the trash. This is because you know that the information inside is most likely from someone trying to sell you something or communicate information that is important to them, but not specific to you.

On the other hand, if you receive an overnight package from FedEx, you are likely to open it right away. The information is perceived as so important and time sensitive that the sender was willing to rush the delivery. The information inside becomes immediately more important, even though you do not know the contents of the package. The same holds true if the letter is sent in either a large envelope or in a fine linen envelope and addressed specifically to you.

The key point here is that if you perceive information to be important to you personally, you are more likely to pay attention.

Now imagine you receive a high-quality linen envelope in the mail and your name and address are correct, but there is no return address. You are likely to open it out of curiosity. If the first sentence says, "Our organization wants to sell you 10 music CDs for a dollar," you would likely throw it away.

It is not that you do not like music or do not purchase music CDs. You would probably throw it away because the organization is trying to sell you something that you do not need at the moment.

However, if the first sentence says, "Recognizing that you appreciate (insert your favorite artist)'s music, we are excited to introduce a series of this artist's newly recorded music currently not available in stores," your attention will be piqued, and you will likely read the next sentence.

In both scenarios, the distribution company is trying to sell you 10 music CDs for a dollar. But in the second approach, the effort is made to create a compelling reason to want to know more about the product by making it more relevant to you.

In the first scenario, the distribution company is confident that its offer of 10 music CDs for a dollar is such a great deal for consumers that it is not necessary to make it meaningful to the consumer. The company believes that the value alone creates the compelling reason to read further. It is also true that 99.9 percent of the people who receive this kind of mail report that they throw it away without even reading it.

Why?

Because people like to buy, not be sold. In order to buy something, you must need or want it. If no need exists, you are not buying; you are being sold something. When you go to the grocery store with a list of items needed for the kitchen, it feels good to be able to cross off each item and fulfill your needs. Now imagine that when you get home, the phone rings and a telemarketer tries to sell you long-distance service that you do not need. That is aggravating, not satisfying.

For hiring managers to read your cover letter, you must identify their needs and use your letter to address the solutions.

Most poorly written cover letters sound like the distribution company that believes its offer is so strong it stands on its own and does not need to relate to you. The distribution company believes that you will automatically act on this special offer, even though it does nothing to make the offer meaningful to you.

Poorly written cover letters focus on your agenda and communicate the following information:

I am responding to the advertised position.

I am interested in this position.

I have developed strong skills through my past employment experiences.

I want to interview for the job.

Please call me.

Notice in this example every sentence starts with "I" and is focused on the writer's wants and interests. It is saying to the employer, "My wants and needs are important for you to know, and once you understand what I am looking for, you should reach out to me and help me achieve my goals."

This type of cover letter does not answer any of the questions relevant to the employer. It does not create a need or describe the solutions you will provide. In fact, it puts the responsibility of your career search on the employer.

A well-written cover letter addresses the specifics of the organization, the position, the timing, and the action steps you will take to facilitate the process.

Here's how to construct a great cover letter.

PARAGRAPH ONE: WHY ARE YOU INTERESTED IN THIS ORGANIZATION?

Recognizing (organization) as a leader in the (industry), I am committed to joining an organization that has an established reputation for delivering high-impact solutions. My experience as an operations executive within this field may be of value as you engage in a search for a new member of your senior management team. I offer over 10 years of progressive advancement in (industry), serving in vital leadership roles, including . . .

PARAGRAPH TWO: WHY THIS POSITION?

(Organization) will benefit from a results-oriented and dedicated executive with demonstrated success in (input parts of the desired position's description). My qualifications not only meet your requirements, but they also provide you with (soft skills like team building, communication, leadership, diversity). Several notable achievements that speak directly to your needs are the following:

(Select three statements from your résumé most applicable to the specific position.)

- Bullet
- Bullet
- Bullet

PARAGRAPH THREE: WHY NOW?

At this juncture in my career, having successfully achieved the corporate goals and objectives set forth by my employer, I am in a position to leverage the leadership skills and innovative thinking capabilities I have developed over the years and apply them as the new (position title), adding immediate and significant contributions to (Organization).

PARAGRAPH FOUR: WHAT NEXT?

While my enclosed résumé outlines my career progression, there is considerably more to share. I will contact you next week to discuss the opportunity to meet in person. I look forward to learning about the next steps in the selection process and can assure you that my drive, commitment, and enthusiasm will be of great value to your team.

This cover letter example answers the four questions that are most relevant to the hiring manager. It emphasizes the needs of the organization and demonstrates how your skills will provide a needed solution. It positions the hiring manager to buy your skills rather than putting him or her in a position to be sold something.

Cover Letter Customization

The more you customize your cover letter to reflect the specific needs of the organization, position, and industry, the better your cover letter will be. Additionally, focus your cover letter on those elements of your résumé that are most attractive to the organization.

For example, if the position is in sales, you may want to emphasize accomplishments that show not only your sales capabilities but also your relationship skills with key accounts. The possibility of bringing new business with you is very desirable to the hiring manager.

- *Initial contact and development of the Bank One account, resulting in more than $4 million in annual sales and recognition as Kinko's #1 National Account Manager of the Year.*

- *Established and expanded more than 30 major accounts, including The Limited, Inc., Cardinal Health, Nationwide Insurance, and Procter & Gamble.*

If the position is in marketing and you do not have direct accomplishments related to the needs of the position, then focus on the profession itself. Show your knowledge of the profession to align yourself with the needs of the organization.

Creating successful marketing programs is more challenging than ever before. With the constant infusion of emerging technologies in tandem with already existing marketing channels, a marketing professional is faced with unlimited opportunities for business development. My success lies in the ability to evaluate these channels, determine the most appropriate mix of marketing tools, and create campaigns that deliver results.

Cover Letter Format

Cover letters, like résumés, are formal documents; they need to be written on high-quality linen paper, using a letterhead that matches your résumé and no more than one page in length.

When addressing the hiring manager, his or her name and title, if known, should appear in the following order:

Date

Full Name
Title
Organization
Address

Dear Salutation (Mr./Ms.) Last Name:

If you are unable to obtain the names of hiring managers, then address them by their title or as the "hiring manager." The same holds true for executive recruiters and search professionals.

For example:

Dear Human Resources Director:

Dear Executive Search Professional:

Dear Hiring Manager:

Dear Selection Committee:

Dear Search Committee:

Do not use:

Dear Sir:

Dear Sir or Madam:

Dear Sirs:

To whom it may concern:

All of these are too vague and hold no one accountable to respond. At least with a title you can follow up on your campaign by requesting the hiring manager responsible for the search.

Follow-Up on Cover Letters

A cover letter and résumé are only as good as your follow-up. You can send an excellent résumé and cover letter to a hiring manager and it might be read, but chances are that the hiring manager will not take the initiative to contact you. While your qualifications are intriguing, hiring managers may not be in a position to stop their daily operations and discuss career opportunities with you. However, if you make the effort to follow up, they are more likely to agree, due to your persistence and interest. It is important to take the initiative to inquire about the possibility of getting together (and make it clear that their time will be respected and used wisely). This action shows your commitment and true interest in the company.

Cover letters are like hunting dogs. A hunter uses hunting dogs to track down rabbits. Once the rabbit is located, the hunter goes after it and takes aim. Cover letters are used to target and focus your qualifications to a specific employer. But that is not enough; you must go after it and take aim. You will not see a rabbit come to the hunter and state, "I understand you are looking for me." The same holds true with employers. You must follow up and be persistent.

The following examples of network letters and cover letters illustrate the principles described above.

NETWORK LETTER EXAMPLE

678 Smith Street, Columbus, Ohio 43085 • 614.123.4567 h

Date

Name
Title
Company
Address

Dear Network Name:

(Why am I interested in talking to you?)

Recognizing that you have been in the Atlanta business community for over 15 years and have numerous contacts in the financial services industry, I am interested in hearing your advice and opinion regarding the market, since my qualifications and skills are well-suited for this industry.

(Why am I worth talking to?)

I have identified 20 financial services organizations that I am targeting for my current research. I am confident that my education and experience provide the skills these companies are looking for in a new employee. You can help me in my research efforts by providing me with any information you may have about these companies or providing the names of anyone you may know who works (or previously worked) within these organizations. Additionally, you may be aware of similar companies that I have not yet identified to add to my prospect list.

(Why now?)

The financial services industry has always held a great deal of interest for me, and now that I have developed the necessary analytical, research, and business development skills needed to perform successfully in the industry, I am ready to begin interviewing with these companies.

(What next?)

Thanks so much for your help and support. I will call you next week to see if you are available for coffee or lunch. I appreciate your time.

Sincerely,

Candidate Name

NETWORK LETTER EXAMPLE

678 Smith Street, Columbus, Ohio 43085 • 614.123.4567 h

Date

Name
Title
Company
Address

Dear Name:

(Why your company?)

Sandy Smith suggested that I submit my résumé to you in consideration of a pharmaceutical sales representative position. I have had a very successful career with Abbott Laboratories in which I have progressively advanced through the organization and currently serve as an advertising manager.

(Why this position?)

Merck & Co. will benefit from a results-oriented leader who can establish strong business relations, influence decision makers, monitor and assess the competitive environment, and achieve territory sales goals. Throughout my career, I have utilized exceptional communication skills to positively influence and motivate medical professionals and other customers.

While serving as a sales representative in Ross Medical-Nutritional Sales, I was the #1-ranked associate for outbound contacts and generated $3.5 million in annual revenues my first year. Additionally, I have successfully presented high-impact proposals to the executive staff of 10 key accounts nationally that effectively persuaded favorable decisions.

(Why now?)

As a result of my 8 years of clinical background in medical-surgical nursing, I have proven success, building valuable relationships with physicians and other health care professionals. Since I have been consistently recognized by senior management, my peers, and clients for my sales and customer service expertise, I am well-positioned to pursue a sales position for a leading pharmaceutical company. While my enclosed résumé describes my career history, there is considerably more to tell.

(What next?)

I will call you next week to discuss an appropriate time for us to meet and explore my qualifications in greater detail. Thank you for your time and consideration.

Sincerely,

Candidate Name

COVER LETTER EXAMPLE

123 Smith Street, Cleveland, Ohio 44101 • 216.123.4567

Date

Name
Title
Company
Address

Dear Name:

(Why company?)

The recent opening at Ohio Wesleyan University for an assistant controller prompted me to immediately update my résumé for your review. I offer over 15 years' progressive advancement in financial services as well as strong analytical, strategic-planning, and communication skills.

(Why position?)

Ohio Wesleyan University will benefit from a results-oriented leader who can direct financial policy development, contract arrangements, and financial tracking/reporting methods for workflow throughout the university. As my résumé details, I am recognized as a distinguished performer in business management, overseeing 17 offices, managing the budget, monitoring expenditures, and providing risk evaluation, process improvement, and financial analysis to deliver improved financial, performance, and profit results.

(Why now?)

At this juncture in my career, I am seeking an advancement opportunity that will allow me to use my financial skills in a greater capacity. I have progressed to the highest level of professional status within the current organizational structure of my present employer and am interested in further developing interests in the financial industry. I am confident that I can make a valuable contribution to Ohio Wesleyan University.

(What next?)

I will call you early next week to discuss an appropriate time for us to meet and explore career opportunities in greater detail. I look forward to the next step in the selection process, as I will be a great asset as the assistant controller. Thank you for your time and consideration.

Sincerely,

Candidate Name

COVER LETTER EXAMPLE

123 Smith Street, Cleveland, Ohio 44101 • 216.123.4567

Date

Name
Title
Company
Address

Dear Name:

(Why company?)

ABC is widely recognized as an industry leader in _____. I am an attorney in private practice, specializing in complex real estate transactions. After representing many different clients with diverse objectives, I wish to change my focus and join a management team as in-house counsel. I want to concentrate in depth on assisting one client to achieve immediate and long-term goals. Accordingly, I am submitting my confidential résumé to ABC. With ABC's significant real estate presence, I believe we have much to offer each other.

(Why position?)

ABC will benefit from my proven leadership, developed through leading and implementing strategic, measurable change for clients as a real estate partner at Malloy, Jones, & Smith LLP. With this nationally recognized law firm, I have directed major site acquisitions for a variety of regional and national clients, specializing in commercial and industrial property transactions for over 20 years. My accomplishments also include successfully leading a team of 15 attorneys handling the real estate aspects of a massive corporate relocation, structuring transactions over $500 million, and positioning corporations to acquire and build retail operations.

I have consistently ranked in the top 10% of the entire firm's attorneys and first, by a very substantial amount, among real estate attorneys based upon revenues received by the firm for my services. Also, I am listed in *The Best Lawyers in America*.

(Why now?)

My position is highly visible, requiring constant interaction not only with my clients, but also with their business partners, financial advisors, and investors. I would now like to use my experience for the benefit of ABC.

(What next?)

If ABC seeks a candidate with my qualifications, I would welcome the opportunity to discuss ABC's legal needs with you. I will call you next week to discuss how to proceed with your hiring process. Thank you for your time and consideration.

Sincerely,

Candidate Name

COVER LETTER EXAMPLE

123 Smith Street, Cleveland, Ohio 44101 • 216.123.4567

Date

Name
Title
Company
Address

Dear Name:

(Why company?)

Recognizing ABC as a leading consumer goods manufacturing company headquartered in San Diego, I am interested in introducing my qualifications for your review and consideration. I offer over 5 years' experience as a training specialist and corporate training manager with multiple training certifications from internationally recognized instructional design/training programs.

(Why position?)

ABC will benefit from an experienced trainer with notable achievements, including demonstrated expertise in designing, developing, and delivering corporate training courses. In addition, I have over 25 years of experience in quality production and coordination for national and international plant training programs.

(Why now?)

At this juncture in my career, having successfully supported the training and QA needs of internationally recognized leaders such as Glad and Clorox, I am interested in contributing my expertise as either a contracting consultant or part-time trainer, or fulfill a full-time position if one becomes available in the near future.

(What next?)

I will call you to inquire about setting up a meeting to learn more about your current and future training needs. I am confident my drive, enthusiasm, and passion for training will be an asset to your company.

Sincerely,

Candidate Name
Enclosures:

The Play of Your Life is a guide that provides directions for what to do on your stage in order to create a career that feels like play, not work. You have developed a résumé that articulates your value and helps employers to recognize the role you are best suited to play within their organization. Additionally, you have learned how to write an effective cover letter communicating how your strengths and talents are relevant to your prospective employers. The next chapter is dedicated to the production phase of your career development. This is the chapter that fully describes why networks are the most effective way to achieve your career goals and how to create and use your network so that it will produce results for you. Here, you will transcend from the knowing to the doing. In order to turn your work into play, you will need to bring your script alive.

Once you know what you want and you are able to communicate it to others in a powerful résumé, you still have to create the opportunities to introduce yourself. Much as a play just doesn't come to life once a script is developed, so an entire production ensues to prepare for opening night. There are usually a lot of people, many behind the scenes, playing a significant role in launching a performance. The same holds true for a job search. While you will be the only one to walk in for the interview, there will be a lot of people who you had to connect with in order to get in front of the decision maker. It is a production, but absolutely worth it!

The Production

YOU ARE READY to start your job search. You have clearly defined your career goals, using the assessments and exercises in Act One to more fully understand your values, personality preferences, and interests. Next you created accomplishment statements and selected the talents, strengths, and areas of expertise that illustrate your ability to make a significant impact in the profession and industry that suits your goals. Then you wrote a cover letter that prompts prospective employers to want to meet you. So how do you get from knowing what you want and being able to artic-

> *"It is not the strongest of the species that survive, or the most intelligent, but the one most responsive to change."*
>
> —*Charles Darwin*

ulate what you want to having the opportunity to interview for an actual position that meets your career goals? The answer to this question is the central theme of this chapter. It is called the production because where many people get derailed on the path to achieving career success is in career search implementation. Few people understand the dynamics of today's job search process and spend endless amounts of time trying ineffective strategies. After enough failings, they simply give up. This program encompasses all areas of career development to ensure that once you embark on a path to career success, you have all the necessary tools to achieve it. The most essential tool when it comes to conducting your job search is knowing how to network.

Networking

Networking is a production. While most people recognize that networking is the most common way to get offered a position, the vast majority do not know how to produce fruitful results through networking. Studies show that nearly 90 percent of all positions are obtained by being in the right place at the right time. More traditional career search techniques are successful only 10 percent of the time. Responding to advertisements, applying to positions posted on job search engines, using a recruiter or employment agency, and sending a blind résumé directly to a company rarely work.

This may seem surprising, given the popularity of job search engines that proliferate on the Internet. While over 40,000 different job search engines exist on the Internet, fewer than 4 percent of 52 million Americans who searched for jobs on the Internet in 2002 actually obtained jobs through this vehicle, according to a report by Pew Internet and American Life Project.

In fact, some companies are so inundated with résumés via the Web that they have stopped using this resource. When Lockheed Martin won a contract to build the F-35 Joint Strike Fighter, the company received more than 100,000 résumés in 1 week via the Internet! Because of these overwhelming numbers, many companies are reticent about using the Internet as a source for employment candidates.

Also, positions that require a specialty or depth of experience are less likely to be posted in places that attract everyone. These employers know that their ideal candidate is likely to come to them through strategic search methods, which often involve networking.

Networking has become the primary vehicle for career search because of the constant flux of the American workplace. Major shifts in the economy are causing companies to move to a more flexible workforce model. While changing jobs is not a new phenomenon, the frequency with which people change jobs has increased significantly and the changes people are making in their work are more radical than ever before.

In the past it was not uncommon to have the same job for an entire career. Today:

- Nearly one out of three American workers has been with his or her employer for less than a year, and two out of three for less than 5 years, according to the Bureau of Labor.

- Of the 106 million people between the ages of 30 and 59, 1 in 10 will change jobs this year alone.

- College graduate will have 5 different careers and 12 to 15 different jobs within those careers.

The good news is that with this much change, opportunities are occurring all the time. Since people change jobs every 2 to 3 years, companies are constantly hiring and rehiring for positions. *The Play of Your Life* offers a new model for capitalizing on this new workplace.

This chapter provides you with the critical elements for successful networking. It will dramatically change your definition, understanding, and application of this vital element in the career search process. The elements include:

- Differences between an open market and a hidden market

- Mental preparation to contact individuals

- Developing your network

- Assessing the quality and value of your networking

- Tracking your networking progress

Differences between Open Markets and Hidden Markets

An open market is any job posting that is openly posted for the public to see. Classified advertisements, job search engines, and organization Web sites are examples of open markets. A hidden market constitutes all opportunities that exist in the marketplace but are never openly posted for the public. Word-of-mouth referrals, internal recommendations, and recruiters are examples of hidden markets.

While most people recognize the importance of networking, few engage in the process, preferring to search for jobs that are openly posted in the marketplace. To understand why this is the case, it is important to examine the pros and cons of searching for jobs via an open-market strategy versus searching for opportunities via the hidden market. What are pros of conducting an open-market career search?

Pros of the Open Market

EASY

The most attractive reason for conducting an open-market search is that it is easy. Most people know how to get the classified advertisements posted in their Sunday newspaper. Also, the Internet provides over 40,000 different job search engines in addition to all the job search postings available on corporate Web sites.

COMFORTABLE

The second most attractive reason for conducting an open-market search is that it is comfortable. You do not have to leave your own home to conduct a job search this way.

FRONT-LOADED

The third most attractive reason for conducting an open-market search is that it feels very productive and efficient. You can submit your application and credentials for literally hundreds of positions with the click of a button by setting up search agents that notify you of positions that match your qualifications. With e-mail, the Internet, and a fax machine, you can get a lot of résumés out to prospective employers in a very short time. This avenue offers a streamlined approach to distribute your résumé, en masse, to as many openings that fit your profile as possible with very little effort on your part.

WELCOMING

Another attractive reason for engaging in an open-market job search is the fact that you have been invited to submit your qualifications. The advertisements are requesting your information, and you are simply granting their request. It is attractive to be wanted.

TRADITIONAL

A common reason for continuing to engage in an open-market search is that it has worked in the past. At some point in your career, you probably submitted your résumé for a position that was posted in the open market and you received an offer. If it worked in the past, why not continue to use this approach? In fact, in the mid to late 1990s, posting your résumé on the Internet for technology jobs was a great way to get a call from a recruiter offering you fantastic opportunities.

LAZY

A less obvious but important factor in why people cling so strongly to the open-market job search process is that it lets the market determine what career path is most appropriate for them. Instead of having to engage in the self-analysis and introspection you completed in Act One, they simply apply for positions that most closely reflect their past experiences. This way, the market makes the difficult career decisions for them. They do not have to know what they want; they simply do whatever the market advertises as currently available.

ATTENTION DEFLECTOR

Another, less obvious reason for holding steadfast to the open-market search has to do with the need to use it as a coping mechanism. It is far more attractive for people to blame the market on their job search woes than to blame themselves. By relying on the open market to drive their career search, they allow themselves the ability to fault it.

Rejection is a very powerful deterrent that people avoid at all costs. If your job search is not about you and is more about the marketplace, you are not being rejected. The market simply is not providing the right opportunities.

These are powerful pros. In fact, if you were unaware of the cons, which most job search novices are, you would not consider conducting any other kind of search. Why would you not want to do something that is easy, comfortable, and traditional, and lets you be lazy and not held accountable? This question brings us to the cons.

Cons of the Open Market

LIMITING

The most powerful con to the open-market search is the fact that so few opportunities are ever posted in the open market. In general, only 2 out of every 10 opportunities currently available in the marketplace are ever openly posted. While the pros of conducting an open job search are very appealing, the fact that you are reaching such a small percentage of the opportunities that exist diminishes this strategy significantly.

COMPETITION

The second most powerful con to conducting an open-market search is the level of competition that exists among the 20 percent of posted opportunities. Since it is so easy and comfortable to apply for jobs in the open market, these positions are sought after by the vast majority of job seekers. It is not uncommon to hear human resources departments state that they receive between 500 and 1,300 résumés for each position they post in the paper or on job search engines. Also, with the introduction of technologies that allow people to blast their résumé to thousands of job postings on the Internet, many employers receive hundreds of résumés that have no relevance to the actual job description. This frustrates employers and makes sifting through résumés from openly posted positions a negative experience.

JOB LEGITIMACY

Another con to pursuing the open-market search process is the fact that not all jobs posted are filled through this strategy. In fact, many jobs are posted simply to fulfill the corporate policy that requires the company to notify the public of the opportunity. They already have the candidate slated for the position but must still post the position for a set number of business days. This is related to equal employment opportunity laws that require employers to announce an opening prior to filling it. Frequently, people assume that when they respond to advertisements and never hear back, it is because the employer reviewed their qualifications and decided not to interview them. The more likely scenario is that the employer either never actually got to the résumé because it was number 698 of the 700 they received and they had stopped looking after the first 50 or did not review any of them because they never really needed a candidate.

BUREAUCRATIC PROCESS

It is not uncommon for me to hear clients complain about the fact that they do not hear back from prospective employers when they submit their applications and résumés. They say it can take months just to get a postcard from the employer stating that their résumé has been received.

While applying to positions in the open market feels very efficient and fast on the front end, there is usually an enormous wait on the back end. Why does it take so long? For starters, trying to hire someone that comes from an unknown resource requires extra attention and detail to ensure that the person does not pose any liability to the company. Think about it this way. If you were set up on a blind date through the personals, you would probably be more cautious about where you chose to meet that person for the first time and take extra precautions in case you did not feel comfortable with the person. You would also likely take more time before giving too much personal information about yourself and might continue to meet other people on the side until you felt certain that this person was worth your full attention. The same holds true for the job search.

Employers would much prefer to meet a prospective employee that came to them through a referral or warm lead. They are far more cautious when the candidate comes to them cold from a paper or an Internet announcement. While the cost of a bad hire varies according to industry, profession, and location, it is pretty safe to say that the average cost of a bad hire starts at about

$5,700 and goes up depending on how critical the position is to the company. So employers are going to be very cautious about hiring someone they do not know without first doing a thorough background check, a reference check, an analysis, and a comparison of all the candidates before making a decision.

BAD FIT

Another major con to conducting an open-market search is the risk of getting hired into a position that is not a good fit because you let the market decide what positions you should apply for instead of using your own self-analysis to find a match. When you use positions posted in the open market to determine what your next step should be, you often end up asking yourself the wrong questions. The question becomes "Can I do this job?" versus "What career is best suited for me, and how do I introduce my qualifications to the right decision maker?" It is like making an odd pair of shoes fit rather than selecting a pair that are truly comfortable for you.

WORSE PAY

While all openly posted positions do not pay less than hidden-market opportunities, many do. The reason is that employers don't have to pay as much when the competition is so fierce. It becomes a buyer's market, and the buyer is the employer. Employers can and will lowball the offer because if you do not take it, they have hundreds of others who might. Since they have not developed a relationship with you or learned about you through a trusted resource, they have nothing to lose by passing you up and going straight to the next in line.

BAD OPPORTUNITY

Open-market positions are not all bad opportunities either, but again, many are. Why? Because if the opportunity were so attractive, then the employer would probably not have to spend money posting the opportunity in the open market and risk getting a bad hire. Employers always prefer to hire through the hidden market because it does not cost them any money in advertising and they receive candidates from a trusted source. If no one in the company or in the industry would recommend someone they know for the position, it is likely that there is something wrong with the position. It either is underpaid, has no advancement opportunities, reports to an unfavorable boss, or has unrealistic performance goals, or it could be several of these factors combined. Again, not all openly marketed positions are bad opportunities, but if there are so few opportunities in the marketplace and so much talent searching for opportunities, then why would a company have to post a cold advertisement to attract people? Wouldn't there be people already approaching the hiring manager to express their interest? The answer is yes. Hopefully, your interest to know more about networking in the hidden market has increased as a result of learning these cons. What are the pros to engaging a hidden-market search?

Pros of the Hidden Market

OPPORTUNITY

If only 2 of every 10 positions available are posted in the open market, then the other 8 are in the hidden market. The more specialized a position is and the more experience a position requires, the more likely it will exist in the hidden market. Open-market advertising makes the most sense to employers who are trying to attract a broad range of applicants to fill multiple positions or positions that turn over frequently. They want a lot of résumés so they can have people lined up for positions as they become open. This is more applicable to entry-level careers or low-level generalist positions that require little more than on-the-job training. If you possess more than 10 years of experience, are looking for opportunities that compensate near or above a six-figure income, and/or are highly specialized in your profession/industry, then the hidden-market search is even more important for you.

MORE ATTENTION

Another huge pro to engaging the hidden market is that you sidestep a lot of the competition by identifying opportunities that others are not aware of yet. This allows you to stand out among the others and present yourself as a valuable solution, instead of just another one of the masses looking for a job.

BETTER FIT

By strategically positioning yourself for opportunities that are in alignment with what you want to do, you ensure that you receive offers for those positions that match your internal career description.

INCREASED CONFIDENCE

When you engage in a hidden-market search, you are more self-directed and clear about what you want and why you are pursuing these particular prospective employers. Instead of just responding to random positions that pop up in the open market, you direct your energy toward a specific profession, industry, location, and type of organization that meets your internal career description. The very nature of knowing why you want to join a specific company and what makes you a good fit will provide you with confidence that is hard to muster up when you are not committed to the actual search process. You will also have more confidence when talking to prospective employers because they will have been introduced to you through someone in your network. This introduction helps significantly in establishing rapport because you are able to learn more about the company prior to the meeting by talking to the person who made the introduction. In an open-market search, all you have to go on is what they write in the advertisement.

FAST-ACTING

Another great pro to the hidden market is the speed with which offers are extended once an introduction takes place. Unlike in the open market, where employers have to be extremely cautious of the applicants, in the hidden market employers who have been introduced to a prospective employee by another trusted employee want to like this candidate. They approach the interview with the intention of making a positive connection that will lead to an offer. Unfortunately, people seek the immediate gratification that comes from submitting a résumé online to a job opening over strategically positioning themselves to introduce their qualifications to prospective employers through their networks. As a result, they ironically end up taking twice as long to get an offer than if they used their networks.

Not only is the hidden market where most of the opportunities are, but they are most of the well-compensated, good-fit overall better opportunities! So why don't people engage the hidden market? Why is networking such a negative experience for job seekers?

Cons of the Hidden Market

The cons of the hidden market are few; unfortunately, they are extremely powerful deterrents. There are only two essential qualities that must exist in order to operate successfully in the hidden market. The first is a clear understanding of who you are and what you want. Most people were never really taught how to think about their career and manage its progression. This was something employers were responsible for. As a result, making choices about your career can feel overwhelming. The first part of this book is designed to help you tackle this difficult issue. The second is a belief that your talents and skills are valuable resources needed by your prospective employers. Because many people associate who they are with where they work, not having work makes them feel unsuccessful. Trying to network when you do not feel confident is a problem that needs to be tackled before you can navigate the hidden market. The next section discusses both of these qualities in more detail and offers recommendations for strengthening your networking skills by applying what you have learned in the first three chapters.

Networking tends to be an uncomfortable experience for many people because the way to proceed is unclear. This does not have to be the case. To appreciate your own networking needs, it is important to integrate your personality style and strengths into your network. If you are authentic in your networking, it will produce positive results.

A network is simply a vehicle in which two separate entities connect. There is nothing especially good or bad about a network. It is how you perceive the network's purpose and how you operate within a network that gives networking a good or bad name.

When your image of a network is positive, you associate it with terms like:

- Relationship building

- Community

- Systems

- Family

When your image of networking is negative, you associate it with terms like:

- Forced

- Pushy

- One-sided

- Artificial

These negative associations often emerge when you apply a networking strategy that is not well-suited to your personality.

To select the best strategy and method for networking, look carefully at your personality type and current perception of yourself. For example, if you have been going to events that require you to talk with a lot of people whom you do not know and this is not a comfortable situation for you, you will develop negative associations with networking. First, recognize that networking does not have to be a negative experience. For it to change to a positive one, you have to alter the approach you take and the perception you have about yourself. In what follows, I will show you how to use all of this information to help pinpoint your best networking strategy. This will also give important insights about the messages you send to others in a network.

Networking Preferences

As you may recall from the personality assessment discussed earlier, your personality preferences determine the extent to which you enjoy certain activities.

If you possess a preference for extroversion, you may enjoy meeting many different people in a short period of time. You like getting the opportunity to learn a little bit about each one. For an extrovert, it is energizing to interact in fast-paced environments because all the activity is stimulating.

If you possess a preference for introversion, you may like meeting only a few knowledgeable people with whom you can engage in meaningful conversation. You like a conversation that is centered on a common interest or function. If you are an introvert, it is energizing to use knowledge about a specific subject or topic to inform others. This activity taps your expertise and is therefore stimulating.

These different preferences require different strategies for networking.

If you have a preference for extroversion, you may enjoy a "speed-networking" event. In this event, the object is to spend no more than 4 minutes with as many people as possible during a 1-hour session. In this way you glean much basic information to apply to your job search.

However, if you have a preference for introversion, you may find this kind of event appalling and completely "superficial." You appreciate a networking event that caters to an audience of professionals and features a knowledgeable speaker on a topic of interest to all attendees. The participants learn from the speaker and engage in conversation with similar-minded attendees. In this scenario, extroverts would be unnerved by the feeling that they had wasted time, sitting through the whole presentation. They would rather be talking to everyone and getting business cards to send out more résumés!

Rich is a client who made it very clear early in our sessions that networking would not work for him. He was comfortable with the few people he knew and did not want to know anyone else. In fact, one of the first quotes he passed along to me was from Groucho Marx, who said, "I don't want to belong to any club that will accept me as a member." Getting out and talking to people, particularly strangers, was the last thing Rich wanted to spend his time doing. At the same time, he was certainly anxious to secure a senior financial management position within the manufacturing industry, where he had been a valuable asset for over 15 years. Knowing this, I recommended that he not go to unstructured after-hours events that would require him to spontaneously strike up conversations with random people. Instead I asked about what he does like to do.

Rich told me that before he got laid off he had been working on an exciting project at work that used a new financial software program to help integrate the financial records of the companies that his company had acquired. The mergers were great for growth but a complete nightmare in terms of managing financial records. Every company they bought had its own proprietary software, and none of them communicated correctly with their corporate mainframe computer system.

Since Rich had a strong information technology background as well as financial management expertise, he had been selected by the corporate office to lead a special task force in creating a solution. Rich enjoyed describing the issues at hand and the steps he took to remedy the problems. It was clear that he knew a great deal about these challenges, and I asked if this is a challenge faced by other companies similar to his. He said absolutely. At that, I recommended that Rich write an article for the local chapter of his professional association. Professional associations are always looking for articles to put in their newsletters or monthly magazines. As part of the article, I asked him to interview the CFOs from his top prospective employer list and then send them a copy of the article with an appreciation for their time.

With this approach, Rich is doing very strategic networking that plays into his strengths. He created a means of using his expertise about a specific subject to introduce himself to key individuals. This initial contact opened the doors for future conversations. Getting the article published also gave Rich publicity and name recognition without having to physically introduce himself to others all the time. Finally, when asked what he had been doing with his free time, he had a great answer to share.

There is no "one size fits all" form of networking, just as there are no two identical personalities. The best way to develop a networking strategy is to identify your preferences. Use that insight to select activities that will produce positive networking experiences and avoid activities that drain your energy.

To identify your networking preferences, ask yourself the following questions.

- What events have I attended that I enjoyed, and why?

- What type of people do I appreciate?

- Do I prefer interacting with people to brainstorm new ideas, or do I prefer assisting someone in executing a proven method or getting predefined desired results?

- Do I prefer going to events that are focused on tactical strategy and operational efficiencies within my profession/industry, or do I prefer attending events that concentrate on soft skills like communication, diversity, community, and employee satisfaction?

• Do I prefer events that have a clearly defined structure loosely maintained by the coordinators, or do I prefer events that leave a lot of flexibility and time for creative expression, interaction, and spontaneity?

The answers to these questions provide a framework for determining which networking opportunities are going to be enjoyable for you. A networking activity does not necessarily involve large groups of people. A networking event can be a phone conversation with a person who has a similar interest regarding a particular profession or industry.

Judy is another client who developed a successful networking approach because it was in alignment with her personality preferences. Using the insights she learned about herself from the exercises in Act One, Judy decided that the best way to engage a network was to write a letter first to introduce herself and then follow up with a phone call requesting a brief meeting. In this manner, she would not be making a totally cold call, and the letter would help her name to register with the person who answered her phone call. While this is not unique, the way she selected her contacts was. Each week, Judy read the local newspapers and magazines to identify individuals in her professional interest category who were highlighted in the paper as a result of a recent promotion or as a new hire. A lot of companies will submit new hires and promotions as a way of getting free publicity. Judy took the information and wrote a very brief note on her personal stationery that stated:

"Congratulations on your recent career achievement to XX position at YYY company! It is always a pleasure to hear about my colleagues' professional successes, and since I am in the process of exploring a career move myself, your exciting news caught my attention. As an experienced professional with over 15 years in the finance industry with a Fortune 500, I recently made the decision to pursue my lifelong career goal—a leadership role within a nonprofit agency dedicated to serving children. Recognizing that this is clearly a passion for you as well, I would appreciate the opportunity to meet you over coffee in the near future. My business card is enclosed, but I will call you next week to discuss a convenient time. Again, best wishes and congratulations."

What is great about this approach is it gave her a reason to follow up that was not only focused on her agenda. She was calling to compliment her prospect and referred to her as a peer rather than as someone who is more important than she. Judy also took the lead in saying that she would take initiative to follow up. She gave the person a very quick overview of her qualifications so the person knew she was an accomplished professional worth spending time with.

Too frequently people shy away from networking because they are uncomfortable with the process. But creating and using a network can be rewarding and even enjoyable if you take some time to think creatively and choose an approach that fits you.

Preparing to network by selecting activities and engaging processes that are in alignment with your personality and strengths is just one important element in experiencing success with your network. Your confidence level also plays an essential role in whether networking is a productive, positive experience or a negative one. Confidence is largely influenced by life events, both past and current. When you undergo a major life change, whether by choice or not, confidence can diminish.

If you identify yourself as unemployed, downsized, riffed, terminated, laid off, retired, or in transition, you are likely to feel less valuable than when you possessed a job title. If you are a graphic designer currently in a career search, and you say, "I used to be a graphic designer with X company, but now I am unemployed," you communicate that you are no longer a graphic designer. But you are still a graphic designer. You are simply no longer a graphic designer for that particular company.

Since it is common in society to tie your identity to the company for which you work, when that tie is severed, you feel you have nothing to offer and are in a position of need. Feeling needy is dangerous because it impedes your confidence. As a result, your ability to establish relationships that produce opportunities is diminished.

When you are struggling with your current situation, even the simplest questions can be extremely stressful. The first question that invariably causes stress is "What do you do?" or "What do you want to do?"

It is vital to remember that your career search is about where you are going. It is future-focused. When asked about what you do by someone you meet, always answer the question in the present or future tense, not the past tense.

Even if you do not have a clearly defined career goal at the time, it is important to show people that you are action-oriented and confident in your process. When people think that you are making a concerted effort, they are more likely to offer you suggestions. When you are positive and excited about your career search, people are more helpful and even go out of their way to help.

Here are suggestions for how to respond to the "What do you do/want to do?" question:

- I am currently researching companies.

- I am exploring several industries.

- I am in the process of conducting a series of informational interviews.

- I am working on a project that will allow me to clearly define my next career path.

- I am engaging my personal network to help identify a target list of companies.

- I am pursuing new opportunities that capitalize on my recent management experience.

Notice how these statements contain action-driven words like *researching*, *pursuing*, *conducting*, and *working*. They establish focus and direction, which helps people connect with you in order to offer guidance and support.

If you do have a clearly defined career goal and are asked, "What do you do?" say:

- I'm looking for an opportunity to contribute my skills, abilities, talents, and experience in the XYX industry as an ABC professional for a leading company such as XXX, YYY, or ZZZ.

This statement is focused on how you add value to a future employer. It very clearly and succinctly presents a vision. As a result of this 10-second pitch, the listener knows the industry, profession, type of company, and expertise that will allow you to achieve career success.

Do not say:

- I am unemployed right now.
- I was recently downsized.
- I was let go.
- I am in transition.
- I got fired.
- I am not doing anything right now.
- I do not know what I am doing.
- I am not sure.

Even though one or more of the statements above may be true, they make it difficult to create a network that produces positive results. The listener is focused on what happened to you or your current state of indecision. These statements are appropriate if you are looking for emotional support. If you want to establish a relationship for the purpose of commiserating over "tough times," then use one these statements. However, if attracting sympathy is not your goal, then keep all negative information to yourself.

People will ask you, "What happened?" The same principles apply. Frame your response to the question so that the focus will transfer to what happened to the company, not to you.

Say:

• My previous employer went through some internal changes, which have prompted me to reevaluate my career path, and I am now looking for an opportunity where I can contribute my skills, abilities, and experiences to . . .

Or:

• My previous employer was faced with extremely difficult decisions to reduce budget as a result of the tough economy. The changes opened the door for me to explore opportunities in the XYZ industry as an ABC professional for a leading company such as XXX, YYY, or ZZZ.

When you perceive being in transition as making you less valuable, you make others believe you are less valuable and your ability to establish a network fails.

If you hear yourself saying, "When I get my life back . . . ," "When I get through this . . . ," "When I get back on my feet . . . ," you send a negative message that you are not contributing. This message sabotages your ability to build a network.

The reality is that you have incredible value to offer at all times. You have the ability to stand on your own two feet regardless of the day, the circumstances, and the variables surrounding you.

Changing jobs, while more common now than ever before, is one of the biggest changes you will undertake. The chance of feeling negative about yourself is even more pronounced when the choice to make a change is not your own. As a result, it is very important to take a personal assessment about how you honestly feel about the change and prepare yourself to deal with your emotions prior to beginning a job search. Too frequently, people forge right into their search for a new position, and when they connect with a member of their network or a potential employer, their conversation is peppered with frustrations. The negative feelings they did not deal with up front come through in their nonverbal conversation and make the listener uncomfortable. In outplacement counseling, it is recommended to wait a minimum of 48 hours after a termination before talking with prospective employers about potential opportunities.

When you experience negative feelings during career change, your feelings must be addressed before a healthy network can be engaged. If you skip this process, you will become your own worst enemy and can actually damage your network. I would rather you not network at all, and hold off on talking to people outside of close family and friends, than start

> *"Delay is preferable to error."*
> —*Thomas Jefferson*

networking before you are ready. The process for repositioning the way you think about yourself is not easy, and there isn't one formula that works for everyone. However, just recognizing when you are feeling down is a huge advantage in beginning to adjust your confidence.

The following are several recommendations to consider if you struggle with self-confidence:

- Do not isolate yourself. Engage a support network of people close to you that can offer positive experiences, love, and friendship.

- Find ways to contribute through volunteering or community service. Contributing to others helps reinforce the reality that you are needed and valued, and that you have many gifts to offer.

- Put your experience in perspective. Keep in mind that people, on average, change jobs every 2 to 4 years. One in every three employees has been with an employer for less than 1 year. Therefore, you are obviously not alone in your transition.

- Recognize that change, while uncomfortable, generally leads to a position better than the one the person held prior to the change. Sixty-eight percent of the people surveyed from outplacement firms said they were happier in their new positions than in their past careers. They also reported finding a better fit for their skills and experiences.

- Pay attention to your language. When you hear yourself saying, "The problem is . . . ," change it to "I am looking for a solution to. . . ." When you hear yourself say, "That will not work because . . . ," change it to "The issue I have been facing is. . . ." Start monitoring what you say and think. When it is negative, restate it in a positive to reposition the challenge you are facing.

- Give yourself a break. Change is hard. You will burn through energy at twice the rate during change. Don't require the same level of productivity from yourself that you achieved at work when the roles and functions were clearly defined and more routine.

- If you think you are too old to be out searching for a new and exciting career, ask yourself how old you will be in 10 years if you do not give yourself permission to go out and find something fulfilling and meaningful. Time goes on with or without you, so you might as well jump in and get the most out of it.

How to Develop Your Network

Developing an effective network requires planning and strategy. You now have an understanding of the preparation needed to engage in the networking process. This section provides the process for building a framework for your network.

You start a network by engaging people you know formally and informally. Your network is not a list of all the people you are going to contact for career search purposes. It is simply a process of brainstorming that allows you to think of people you have not thought of in years and to see connections among them. You do not need to like everyone on this list or let all of them know you are conducting a career search. Each name may prompt you to think of someone who can be more useful in your career search. After you write the first draft of your list, go back and ask yourself, "Who introduced me to this person?" "How did I come to know this person?" This will help you identify even more people you have not thought about in a long time, as well as identify the people in your network that are Power Networkers. Your Power Networkers are the people on your list who have played a role in introducing you to a lot of people. For example, Nettie is a professional colleague who does instructional design for my company. She is also one of my Power Networkers because she is responsible for introducing me to most of the people I know in Atlanta, Georgia. Since I know this, when I need a contact in an industry that is unfamiliar to me, I contact her before others in my network because I know she is likely to know someone. The same is true for Jay, a fellow career counselor. He is the reason I know most of my peers in Atlanta, but it was not until I created the list and went back through it to identify how I'd met all those people that I realized that Nettie and Jay are my Power Networkers.

Developing a network is not just about who you know. It is also about who the people you know, know. Most people know about 250 people at some level, either formally (family, friends, associates, neighbors) or informally (former classmates, past employees, friends of friends, acquaintances, distant relatives). You will realize when you do the exercises that you have come into contact with a lot of people throughout your life.

The exciting news is that even if you cannot think of 250 people, there is a good possibility that the people you do know will know 250 people. If you can think of 250 contacts and each contact can think of 250 people they know, you will have access to 62,500 people!

Jog your memory to identify your 250 people by doing the following:

• Create a timeline of your life to date. Start at the beginning—include schools, friends from school, activities in school, sports you participated in as a child. Look through photo albums and class yearbooks, college mementos, and anything related to your childhood, adolescence, high school, and college.

• Review your résumé and think about every job and every project you have ever worked on from the beginning of your career. Consider clients, customers, vendors, and consultants who you have worked with.

• Think about every resource you use in your personal life. Who do you know at the grocery store, pharmacy, dry cleaners? Think of your neigh-

1		23		45	
2		24		46	
3		25		47	
4		26		48	
5		27		49	
6		28		50	
7		29		51	
8		30		52	
9		31		53	
10		32		54	
11		33		55	
12		34		56	
13		35		57	
14		36		58	
15		37		59	
16		38		60	
17		39		61	
18		40		62	
19		41		63	
20		42		64	
21		43		65	
22		44		66	

bors (past and present), clubs you belong to, people you have dated, people you receive e-mail from or send e-mail to, activities you are involved in (aerobics, art class, sailing).

• Now survey your contact list and ask yourself, Who do these people know? Who are their spouses, friends, colleagues, coworkers? Where did they go to school? What clubs do they belong to? And so on, until you have completely exhausted every single person you know.

EXERCISE: NETWORK GENERATOR

Identify your network in the boxes below.

67	89	III
68	90	112
69	91	113
70	92	114
71	93	115
72	94	116
73	95	117
74	96	118
75	97	119
76	98	120
77	99	121
78	100	122
79	101	123
80	102	124
81	103	125
82	104	126
83	105	127
84	106	128
85	107	129
86	108	130
87	109	131
88	110	132

While the network exercise may not appear to list the right people for you to contact, do not take the chance of missing the obvious. There is a saying in advertising that goes, "Only the dumbest of mice would hide in a cat's ear, but only the wisest of cats would think to look there." We are creatures of habit and get into comfortable routines that center around our own little nucleus of close friends and family. As a result, most people, when asked how many people they know, respond with a far smaller number than is true. They are simply not thinking about those people.

Here is an example. Last year at a workshop, I asked a participant what career path she was pursuing, and she said, "Day care." I asked her to tell me more, and she said she was interested in running a day care facility. I asked if she wanted to acquire an existing one, work as an employee for someone else's day care, start her own, or buy into a franchise. She stated that she was interested in the franchise option. I asked her if she knew which franchise she wanted to buy, and she said she was exploring a relationship with Tiny Tykes. As soon as she said the name, it struck me that about a year earlier I had counseled a women named Nora Williams who had left the telecommunications industry and bought a Tiny Tykes franchise. Immediately I offered to track down Nora's contact information and see if she would be willing to share her experience with the workshop participant. Now, I would not have thought of Nora in a million years because she is not a part of my close nucleus of friends and family. But she is in my database and a great contact for this participant.

There are people right in front of you, each of whom knows about 250 people who you do not know. Could they be a resource for you just by virtue of the introductions they may be able to make for you? Once you have developed your network list, your ability to reach someone else through this list grows exponentially by 250 for each of the 250 people on your list.

This idea of exponentially growing your networking list is the foundation of another concept, referred to as six degrees of separation, which states that you are only six people away from anyone else by using your network. Numerous studies have been conducted to determine if this theory works. Every time it has been tested, two totally unrelated people anywhere in the country were connected to each other within six contacts, on average.

In developing your network list, look for clues and connections that may help you reach a person you want to meet but do not have access to or know. You may know that your neighbor is in the medical field and think, "She cannot help me because I need access to people that are in academia." However, when you share your professional objective with her, you may find out that her aunt is a professor. The aunt may be able to assist you in connecting to the appropriate person within your particular specialty.

When you understand these principles, it becomes clear why nearly 90 percent of career opportunities are found through networking. You live in a very small world. The ability to use this network comes down to your willingness to reach anyone you want through only six contacts.

You are probably thinking, "If it is really this simple, why does it seem difficult?" The concept is simple, but making it work for you takes planning, strategy, and finesse.

Communicating Effectively to Your Network

Even though you are closely connected to everyone else, you may not necessarily know how to communicate with people in a manner that produces desired results.

It is human nature for people to gravitate toward people who are like them. When you expand your network by tapping into someone else's network, it requires that you find something in common with them. This commonality allows you to establish a connection.

In order to do this, look for common denominators between yourself and the person. Do you have anything in common regarding the:

• Industry

• Profession

• Dynamics of the organizations where you have both worked

• Status within the organizational structure

• Community activities

• Family

• School

Communicating with your network is more about the people in your network than it is about *you*. Using a network effectively requires you to know what the people in your network are like and then find something you can offer that is in alignment.

The initial message that you send to your network is extremely important. If you send a message saying, "I need a job, any job," you run the risk of over-whelming your network. The request for a job is so broad that people do not know how to respond in a meaningful way. They either shut down or give you feedback and suggestions that are not useful or relevant.

Also, if you send a message saying, "I am an insurance agent, but I want to be a teacher because Georgia needs teachers. Can you help me?" your net-work will pass along the message that you are X but want to be Y. This is no longer networking; it is a request for help. Unlike an effective networking message, people receiving this request are not as readily in a position to help you change careers.

Consider changing the message to "Teaching has been a long-time interest and passion throughout my life; educating my clients has been the aspect of my career that I most enjoy. What teachers in your life had the most profound impact on you? I'd like to talk to them. Do you know how I could reach them?" Now you send a message that says, "I teach. I want to know what teacher you respect. I want to talk to that teacher." People can respond to that clear request.

If you feel like you have exhausted your network, it is probably because you are not actually networking; you are asking for help. As you plan your networking strategy, devise a set of questions that create opportunities to network, as opposed to questions that request help.

Networking Questions

- What associations have you been involved with over the years? Do you know who the current association director is or how to find that information? What did you get out of the membership?
- What recruiters have you used in the past?
- Who would you say has been a mentor to you in the profession/ industry?
- Who would you say are the real mavericks within the field?
- What previous companies have you been involved with? How do they compare with where you are now?
- Is XYZ organization involved with any specific cause in the community?
- Where can I get a list of the board of directors?
- Who are the major players within the organization/industry/profession?
- What are the organization's major initiatives?
- What are the organization's strengths?
- What industries are similar?
- Who are the organization's competitors?

- What vendors does the organization use for complimentary services/ products?

- What is the organization's culture?

- What advice would you give someone exploring opportunities within this profession/industry?

- Who do you most respect within this organization/profession/industry?

- What trade journals/periodicals/subscriptions are relevant within this profession/industry?

- What do you wish you had known about the organization/profession/industry before getting into it?

- What part(s) of my résumé need(s) to be changed in order to better reflect how my skills apply to this organization/profession/industry?

Informational Interviews

The answers to the above questions are not available on the Internet or in a book. Through informational interviews, you will tap into a greater knowledge about your target organizations, fields, and positions than you have through research.

Informational interviews help you establish a knowledge base for identifying commonalities with people within your target organization, profession, or industry. All of the questions listed above will funnel your network by moving you from six degrees of separation to five degrees, then four degrees, on down to one degree—the actual decision maker. This is the person who is in a position to present an opportunity to you.

Informational interviews are also a nonthreatening way to build relationships with potential employers. Since the objective is to learn about the organization, industry, or profession, people are confident that they can help you. Setting up informational interviews is actually fairly easy when your true objective is to obtain information and guidance. However, if people think you are calling them because you want their help in obtaining a job within their organization, they may be guarded and less likely to meet with you.

There are generally four reasons that people refuse to engage in an informational interview:

1. I do not have time.
2. I do not think I can help you.
3. I am not in a position to hire anyone. You should talk to Human Resources.
4. My organization does not allow us to discuss interpersonal or organizational issues outside of the organization.

Overcoming Objections

When people say, "I do not have time," they feel stressed by so many other priorities and do not see your request for information as a priority. Make yourself very accommodating to their schedule, suggesting several meeting dates that are a week, 2 weeks, and even 3 weeks out. Suggest meeting at their office or before work for coffee at a convenient location on their way to work. Clarify that you will respect their time and only need 15 to 20 minutes. If this feels uncomfortable for you, do not push yourself to make the appointment. Simply thank them and ask if they can recommend someone who might be willing to share advice and support as you explore options in this particular industry.

When they say, "I do not think I can help you," they are likely uncomfortable with providing advice on how to find a job. Let them know that you called them simply because they are in the industry that you are exploring and want to obtain their opinion of the marketplace from an insider's perspective. Use a qualifying statement to clarify your intent.

You might say, "Perhaps you cannot help me. I am interested in talking to someone with experience in (profession/industry). My research produced your name as someone who fits that criterion. Are you not in this (profession/industry)?" If they say they are but are still not sure how they can help you, follow up by stating that you are researching the industry and have developed a list of 10 questions that you would like to discuss with them. Note that you will require only 15 minutes of their time and will meet at their convenience.

When people say, "You must be looking for HR; I do not hire people," they think you are calling them for a job. Redirect and say you apologize for misleading them. You are not looking to meet with them about a job; you are calling to request help with your research.

When people say that organization policy does not allow them to discuss the current organizational situation with outsiders, apologize for the misunderstanding. State that you certainly respect their privacy and you are not seeking any proprietary information. Rather, you are looking to discuss the general profile of the industry and the professional advice they could share based on their experiences.

Most people are willing to offer their advice, opinions, and feedback, but if they feel you are asking for a job, they are likely to use these excuses to avoid feeling pressured to do something they may not feel compelled to do or be able to do.

Networking allows you to tap into career opportunities that are emerging everywhere. The definition of "job" is changing, and the way you search for one is changing, too. Working for one employer in a specific job for a long period of time is no longer a realistic expectation. A job task performed around projects, as opposed to a position, which a person performs full-time.

Today:

- 1 in 10 people is employed under an alternative arrangement.

- More than 24 million people are self-employed.

- 1,500 people become self-employed every day.

By networking, you can tap into more opportunities and possibilities than ever before; the challenge is harnessing these opportunities! Creating opportunities is a relatively new skill. A leading business school did a study showing that its graduates did well during their first 10 years of employment. After the first 10 years, however, they were overtaken by a more successful, streetwise, pragmatic group. What the professor who conducted the study realized was "We taught them how to solve problems, not recognize opportunities."

The massive changes being driven by new-product development, globalization, and technological advances are creating more opportunities for new career paths to emerge, and the pace of these changes is increasing.

Two examples of this change:

- In 1981, 2,700 new products hit the grocery shelves. In 1996, that number swelled to nearly 20,000—a new product every half hour.

- The International Telecommunications Union identified that while it took 74 years for the telephone to reach an audience of 50 million people, and 13 years for television, it took only 4 years for the World Wide Web to achieve the same.

Networking is the best way to take advantage of the opportunities born every day. The process outlined in The Production allows you to confidently, clearly, and strategically connect with opportunities that allow you to perform center stage. Once you capture these opportunities, you have to convince the hiring managers that you are the shining star they have been waiting for. Now that you know how to create and use your network effectively, you will be able to produce opportunities to interview. Learning how to interview for a career that promises to be rewarding and aligned with your values, preferences, and interests is a process, like every step leading up to this chapter. Interviewing for positions, just like auditioning for a play, requires you to rehearse and know your lines. It is not the time to figure out what you should be saying; it is the time to beautifully communicate what you have already thought about and planned to say. The next chapter, The Audition, offers valuable information and guidance to ensure that your interviews lead to an offer that achieves your goals.

The Audition

BEFORE AUDITIONING FOR a play, a performer must know the script and what the director wants in the production. The same premise holds true for performing well in interviews. In an audition, actors put forth their best performance in order to be selected to play the role in the play. When you go for an interview, the prospective employer is expecting your very best as well. Also, just as auditions are contrived because the actor

> *"Nature has given men one tongue and two ears that we may hear twice as much as we speak."*
>
> —*Epictetus*

is only showing a piece of his performance abilities in a short clip, the interview is the same. You have only a very short period of time for which you are judged on your entire career. The audition is a vehicle where actors must be perfect if they expect to be selected for the lead part. Now that you have found yourself center stage by completing the exercises and assessments in Act One, it is time to learn how to express your talents and strengths so that you are selected to perform in the role that is most true to you. This chapter describes:

1. What employers are truly assessing during an interview and how you can build your performance around these key elements
2. The questions you will be asked, both positive and negative, and the questions you will ask the interviewer
3. Interview attire
4. A list of sample interview questions

Auditioning is not just reading the lines from a script. It requires a performance that ignites the producers' imagination and lets them know that you are capable of implementing their vision. Interviewing, like auditioning, requires preparation and conditioning. You must know your part and how it relates to the rest of the cast.

What Employers Really Want

Employers want to hire candidates who understand their organization's goals and objectives. They want to hire people who offer solutions and contributions. They want you to listen to them, understand them, and commit to acting in their best interest. They want you to be focused on the company, not yourself.

You may not know that more offers are extended in an interview when the interviewer talks more than the interviewee. Yes, that's right. More offers are extended when you get interviewers to share about themselves and the company than when they spend their time listening to you talk about yourself.

How do you get the interviewer to talk about the company rather than drill you with endless questions?

1. Become a "consultant"—offer insights and value.
2. Use bridging questions—prompt for feedback and advice.

Become a Consultant

Become a "consultant" as quickly as possible by positioning yourself as someone who offers insights and value relevant to the company's current needs. When interviewers ask a question, answer it, and then offer an analogy from your own experience that shows the value your background can bring the company. Here is a sample interview for a small start-up firm.

Q: What kind of leader are you?

A: Having worked for several fast-paced start-ups as well as large corporations, I've found that my leadership style has always been easily incorporated into growth-oriented companies experiencing aggressive change. I am strategic in thinking and expert at building teams that buy into the corporate vision. I am also dedicated to supporting the team by giving it the tools and resources it needs to really excel. I realize that in small, fast-paced companies, a good manager knows the important distinction between managing projects and leading people. Since your company has experienced so much growth and change in the last 6 months, I think it would be really valuable to . . . (offer an insight relevant to the company based on your experience and allow the interviewer to respond).

Use Bridging Questions

If opportunities to serve as a consultant do not emerge naturally, use questions that bridge your past accomplishments to the company's present issues.

This stimulates the interviewer to share information with you. After your initial response to a question from the interviewer, pose a question of your own about a specific functional area.

- Is this the kind of information you were looking for?

- Based on what I have said, how will this experience be of value here?

- Could you tell me how these skills will be important to this position?

- Would you like additional details about this experience that may relate to your specific needs?

- Is this the kind of detail you are looking for?

- Has this (function area) been a challenge for your company/department in the past?

- What I hear you saying is . . . Do I have that right?

- What kind of personal attributes are most valued here?

Bridging questions not only open opportunities for interviewers to engage and share perspectives; they also demonstrate good active listening skills.

How Employers Make Hiring Decisions

Interviewing is like a chess game. It is not the person with the most assets who wins. It is the person who uses his assets most skillfully who wins. The reality is that you can be the absolute best candidate for a position and still not get the offer. The way to consistently get the offer is to influence interviewers to believe that you are the best candidate. Having talent, genius, and education is not enough; you have to show the interviewer you have these attributes.

Interviewers base hiring decisions more on how they feel about you than about what you actually say in an interview. It is important to realize that what you say is not the only factor in interviewing well; how you present what you say is even more important.

Ensuring Employers Feel Good about You

Here are some ways to ensure that your interviews go well.

PREPARE!

The interview is not the time to think about what to say. The interview is the time to focus on presenting the information that you have prepared for the interview. Do your thinking and planning before the interview. Interviewing well requires preparation.

When you are called to schedule an interview with a prospective employer, ask questions to assist yourself in preparing effectively.

1. Could you please give me an indication as to the amount of time I should expect to spend at your organization?
2. Who will I be interviewing with?
3. Will I be interviewing with each person separately or as part of a panel?
4. What are the name and title of each person I will be meeting?
5. In what capacity would I be interacting with each of these people if offered the position?
6. Is there an organizational chart I could review prior to the interview?
7. How long has the present director been with the organization?
8. How many candidates have been selected for this round of interviews?
9. Will there be any particular tests or additional forms I will need to fill out when I arrive or during the interview process?
10. While I have the description of the position from the newspaper (or wherever you learned of the position), is there any additional information on

file about the position, the performance criteria, and the organization that I could request for review in preparation for the upcoming interview?

All of these questions allow you to get a better picture of what to expect during the interview. Knowing the time frame, type of interview, backgrounds of the interviewers, and expectations of the interview allows you to prepare effectively.

- If you know that three people will be interviewing you, you know to bring multiple copies of your résumé.

- If you know who is interviewing you, you will be more likely to deduce what types of questions they will ask you.

- If you know how many candidates and what stage of the interview process they are currently in, you will know what type of questions they will ask. Based on this information, you can plan accordingly.

This sort of preparation will help you engage the interviewers and build their feelings of confidence in you.

KNOW THE MOST DESIRED ATTRIBUTES

There have been many surveys conducted to assess the attributes hiring managers desire most in candidates. The survey takers discovered that the most important elements were the intangibles, the feelings the interviewer had about the candidates.

Personal	Professional
Drive	Reliability
Motivation	Honesty/Integrity
Energy	Pride
Chemistry	Dedication
Confidence	Analytical Powers
Determination	Listening Ability
Communication	Responsibility

These personal attributes are experienced through your interaction with interviewers, not through what you actually say. When you are prepared, you can spend the interview creating an environment where interviewers observe your confidence. You will naturally exhibit more energy and enthusiasm, and a better communication style.

Prepare for the interview as you would prepare for an exam. If you study the material that will be on the exam in advance, you feel confident about your ability to ace the test. As a result, you are probably more excited to get to the test and show your knowledge. There is less anxiety associated with it because you know you will do well. The converse is also true. If you are not prepared, anxiety is produced and it is even harder to concentrate.

FEEL GOOD ABOUT YOURSELF— IT'S CONTAGIOUS!

The most important element of preparation is for you to feel good about yourself. If you enjoy the interview, then you are more likely to make interviewers feel the same way. You create an atmosphere that offers an opportunity to exchange ideas.

In the musical *Annie*, the lead sings, "You're never fully dressed without a smile." Always remember, smiles and laughter are a universal language. They are contagious. It is hard to smile too much in an interview. More often than not, interviewees are so serious that they do not smile at all.

Feeling good about yourself and being prepared are two important steps in acing the interview. A third important element is recognizing that people like people who are like them.

EMPHASIZE COMMONALITIES

People gravitate toward people who have things in common with them and who share similarities, ideas, and interests.

Understanding this can help you to perform well in an interview. A simple technique is mirroring interviewers' nonverbal communication styles. Another technique is to demonstrate that your experience is of interest to a particular company. These approaches to interviewing help underscore your similarities. The following list provides insight into some of the accomplishments that companies have in common—activities they value and want you to value, too. Underscore these during your interview to demonstrate your similarity to a company.

COMMONALITIES—UNIVERSAL LANGUAGE OF BUSINESS

- Saved time
- Generated revenue
- Increased profits
- Reduced costs
- Streamlined a process
- Improved efficiency
- Created a policy/procedure
- Upgraded a system
- Met corporate goals
- Outperformed competition
- Penetrated a new market
- Identified an untapped niche
- Developed a high-performance team
- Increased productivity

You can ace the interview by understanding and incorporating these three suggestions into your audition:

1. Stimulate interviewers to share their perspective on the position, company, and professional interests by applying bridging questions and acting as a consultant.
2. Prepare in advance for your verbal responses so that you can concentrate on exhibiting nonverbal behavior. This allows the interviewer to experience your personal attributes and feel confident about you.
3. Demonstrate that your personal qualities fit the position by understanding universal commonalities and adapting your style to the hiring manager's style.

Most Effective
Interview Answers

From Lincoln's homespun tales to Aesop's fables, storytelling plays an integral role in the fabric of our country, tying our past to our present.

People remember through association, by connecting one experience with another. Too many interview answers use vague examples or link a string of buzzwords together. This might sound impressive, but the information will be forgotten by the end of the day. Interviewers need to envision what is being said and associate the meaning.

People hear buzzwords, but stories make people listen. When telling a story, you not only associate their experience and your own; you also become more animated and engaging, and smile more. Interviewing in this way will also be more enjoyable, since you will be able to express the attributes you have that are desired by employers.

Interviewers not only want to know that you have the capability; they also want you to demonstrate that you have obtained results. Sharing your results and accomplishments in stories is essential. It communicates your value in a way that increases confidence in interviewers and helps them to remember your strengths.

Stories have a form: a beginning, a middle, and an end. A simple way to construct your stories is the BAR approach.

Background—Summarize the project/problem you faced.

Action—Describe the actions you took to achieve results.

Results—Describe the results, and quantify them if possible.

By constructing BAR stories, you will raise the bar to a new level of interviewing success! Remember, you are responsible as the storyteller to engage the listener by conveying a positive and enthusiastic attitude.

Answers That Focus on the Organization

Begin by constructing stories that clearly relate to the prospective organization and the position description.

1. Review the position description and identify the following information from it.

   • What are the most important skills required in this position?

   • What are the functions this role will fill in the organization?

2. Take a broader perspective and identify:

   • What are the most important attributes of this profession?

   • What are major initiatives/trends affecting this profession?

   • What are the most important attributes of this industry?

   • What are major initiatives/trends affecting this industry?

Notice that preparation in developing stories starts with a focus on the position you are applying for, not on your past. The interview is more about the experience you bring to the company than it is about you. Therefore, the accomplishments/experiences you highlight with your BAR stories should only be those related to the organization's needs.

Commonality Exercise

Look for commonalities between you and the employer that will connect you to each other.

• What do you have in common with the industry?

• What do you have in common with the profession?

• What do you have in common with the specific organization?

• What do you have in common with the specific position?

Create a metaphor; compare seemingly unrelated concepts, and find similarities between them. For example, take a cat and a refrigerator—both have a place to put fish, both purr, both come in a variety of colors and have a lifetime of about 15 years. You can find similarities between almost any two things. Go through your past experiences and identify commonalties between your experience and the employer. Employers need to see how your past is relevant to them. Identify these areas in advance.

Answers That Highlight Accomplishments Listed on Your Résumé

The next place to turn for interview preparation is your résumé because it is the interviewers' reality of you. As a result, your résumé becomes part of the outline for the interview, and many of the interview questions will be drawn from it.

Use your résumé to develop accomplishment stories. Look at each statement on your résumé and identify how it relates to the universal language of business. Emphasize your results in the stories you develop.

First Impressions

Most employers make up their minds about your candidacy in the first 4 minutes of the interview. Since first impressions are so important, be well-prepared for the first four questions of your interview. Know your introduction and your responses to these questions inside out.

The first four questions are generally some version of the following:

- What can you tell me about yourself?

- Why are you interested in this company?

- Why are you looking now?

- What are your accomplishments?

Answering Questions—
Positive and Negative

Questions are designed to assess your strengths and identify your weaknesses. Positive questions provide opportunities to sell yourself, and negative questions are attempts to screen or narrow the candidate pool.

Positive Questions

Questions about your strengths are asked when interviewers want to know how you differentiate yourself from the rest of the candidates. They want to know you are the best candidate. You should leap on the opportunity and offer a fully engaging story with powerful results. This answer should clearly satisfy the needs and expectations of the company.

Make sure that your answer to a strength question is:

- Relevant

- Recent

- Results-oriented

- Enthusiastic

- Dynamic

- Immediate

Immediate means you do not have to think to answer these questions. When asked about your strengths, you should brim with stories about how you have added significant contributions in your past positions.

When an interviewer asks a strength question, before responding always silently add to the end of the question " . . . and what does this have to do with the company/position?" This strategy ensures that you tie your response to its relevance to the company/position.

Negative Questions

Do not say you have no weaknesses or have nothing negative to say about your career experiences when asked directly to share them. If you tell interviewers that you have successfully hit the bull's-eye every time, they will only come away believing that you are standing too close to the target or not being truthful.

> *"The greatest of faults is to be conscious of none."*
> —*Thomas Carlyle*

Discussing challenges and obstacles you have faced during your career is an element of an interview that cannot and should not be avoided when brought up by interviewers. Your focus should not be on the challenge or problem itself, but on what you learned from it and how it made you a stronger professional.

Edison discovered 1,800 ways *not* to build a lightbulb before finding the right way. He learned how to build a lightbulb from his mistakes. Remember, Columbus started out looking for India! Mistakes are not something you should avoid discussing, but maintain your focus on how you have learned and grown from the experiences.

Weakness questions are far more challenging than strength questions. People lose more offers because of poorly managed answers to weakness questions than responses to strength questions.

The first step in preparing for weakness questions is to examine your résumé and identify anything that could be perceived as a weakness. Perhaps the position you are interviewing for wants the candidate to have an MBA and you do not have one. When asked what your weakness is, say, "I'm concerned that it will be considered a weakness that I do not possess an MBA." Immediately add the reasons that the weakness will not have an adverse effect on your job performance by refocusing on your extensive and pertinent experience. They already know you do not have an MBA and still called for an interview. The weakness question gives you an opportunity to diminish any concerns from information in your résumé, and you have not given them any new concerns to consider.

If there is nothing on your résumé that you can use as a weakness, then choose a weakness that is content-focused or technical in nature. This kind of weakness is one you can be quickly trained in if hired. If, however, you are not from the same industry or profession or do not have required education or desired years of experience, then address one of these weaknesses first.

> *"We confess to little faults only to persuade others that we have no great ones."*
> —*François La Rochefoucauld*

Weakness questions are typically asked when interviewers need to narrow down the candidate pool. When you're asked a screening question, your goal is simply to stay in the running. Do not use these questions for lengthy discussions. Keep your answers short, and reposition them to draw on your strengths.

When asked a weakness question, you want to make your answer is:

- Dated
- Unrelated
- Developmental in nature
- Short

- Growth producing

- Delayed

Delayed means that you want to think before responding. It should be difficult for you to identify your weakness. These answers should be short and focused predominantly on what you learned from the experience. Talk about how you have grown and how, when you look back on the experience, you realize it was an opportunity to improve your skills.

At all costs, stay away from giving personality/behavioral traits as weaknesses. These are very dangerous because they are typically the weaknesses that come to mind immediately. Unfortunately, they are also the hardest ones to correct. For example, you may prefer to wait until substantial pressure has developed before getting to work on a project. People like this thrive on the excitement of completing projects just in time. Unfortunately, there are times when this behavior may be interpreted as a weakness. A preference such as this cannot be changed easily and can give the employer reason to doubt your ability to always execute on time.

When asked a weakness question, before responding always silently add to the end of the question " . . . and what have I done to overcome this and grow as a professional?"

Additional Tips in Answering Questions

Keep your answers to 2 minutes, since most adults have an attention span of that length. If you feel yourself talking for more than 2 minutes, pause and make sure you still have the attention of the interviewer. If the interviewer is nodding along with the story, reacting with facial expressions that mirror the tone of what you are saying, then you have more time. If not, take a break from your answer and ask a short question to reestablish interaction. For example, you might say, "Do you know what I mean?"

Restating the Question

When you give an example of your strength by telling a story, always begin by restating the question as part of your answer. While telling stories is a great method to make yourself memorable, it can also be difficult to remember the original question that led to the story. You are more likely to remember the question you are asked if you hear yourself restate it as part of your answer. It will be very uncomfortable for you and the interviewer if you tell a story and then forget why you are telling it.

Direct Answers

Always answer the question you are asked. If you do not know the answer, it is okay to tell the interviewer that you do not know the answer. Explain that you will furnish that information as soon as possible. It is also okay to ask for clarity on the question that has stumped you.

> *"I was gratified to be able to answer promptly, and I did. I said I didn't know."*
>
> —*Mark Twain*

You may say in a very friendly and positive tone, "Wow, I have to admit I am completely caught off guard by that question; could you tell me more about what you are trying to get to?"

This question allows you to stall and think while the interviewer responds. It may also give you more insight as to what they are looking for in the answer and trigger a response for you. If you can't think of an answer, then tell the interviewer, "You have asked an important question and I want to respond appropriately; however, I need to think about what you asked and will provide you my thoughts on (topic) within 2 days."

Salary Requirements

When asked about salary requirements early in the interview process, redirect the interview to your accomplishments versus the money you require. You do not want them focused on your needs before they are committed to needing you. You might say something similar to "I appreciate your interest in knowing my salary needs; however, I want to make sure that I am indeed the best qualified candidate for this position before we discuss money. What do you need to know about my accomplishments to assess whether I am right for you?" If they say that they need to know salary requirements before continuing with the selection process, then provide a broad range. Make it very clear that the salary you require is directly affected by the level of responsibility involved in the position.

It is a good sign when salary requirements are brought up at the end of the interview. This typically means you passed the interview, and now they want to know if they can afford you. At this juncture, it is appropriate to say, "I am very interested in the position and feel confident that we can come to a mutually agreeable offer. Before I can provide a dollar figure, would you please tell me about your benefits package and advancement process? I see this move as a great first step and would like to know how I can grow in this company, since these answers have an impact on my salary expectations." You can also say, "I am very interested in the position and want to make sure I accommodate your pay scales. Is there a budgeted amount in mind for this position?"

Being Overqualified

You may be asked questions about being overqualified. When the market is saturated with specific talent, it becomes a buyer's market. Unfortunately, you may find yourself interviewing for positions for which you are overqualified. As a result, an employer will ask you, "Why are you interested in this position when you are clearly overqualified?" There are several approaches to address this answer.

First, you could redirect and qualify the position by saying, "My understanding is that you are seeking the absolute best candidate for the position, and I am confident that I am that person. My qualifications will allow me to do incredible work for your company."

Second, you could qualify the question by finding out what is really their chief concern. For example, are they concerned that you will continue to look for other opportunities and leave as soon as a higher-paying position becomes available? Are they concerned that you are going to be bored and unchallenged in this role? If this is not the case for you, then it is appropriate to address those particular concerns directly. If, however, you plan to use this position as a temporary move between your last position and your next career move, redirect and go with the first approach.

Asking Questions

While answering questions is a significant portion of the interview, your ability to ask effective questions is just as important.

Pre-Offer Questions

When asking questions in an interview, concentrate on asking "pre-offer" questions, which are ones to ask before you receive a job offer. Post-offer questions are those that you ask before you accept a position that has been offered to you. In a pre-offer stage, your entire focus should be on getting an offer. If you determine during an interview that the position is not a good fit for you, you can always turn down the offer.

If you focus during the interview on whether or not you want the position, you may sabotage the interview without even realizing it. Your doubts may show via nonverbal cues, such as reduced energy and enthusiasm. Concentrate on getting the offer, as opposed to what to do with the offer if you get it.

Pre-offer interviews are not the appropriate time for questions that address your agenda; those are for the post-offer stage. Pre-offer questions need to elicit positive experiences and good feelings.

Selling Yourself through Questions

Your questions provide an opportunity to position yourself favorably in the organization. Do this by asking questions that encourage employers to envision you as an important member of their team. There is a strategy to asking questions that can play an integral part in your success as an interviewee.

A great question to ask is "If selected for this position, what will I need to accomplish in the first 12 months to receive an outstanding performance review?" This question makes the interviewer envision you in the company as a top performer. You actually make that person "see" you as great in order to answer the question.

Asking effective questions can also help you learn about hard-to-research aspects of the organization. It may be difficult to learn about an organization's culture from corporate literature, external research, or the company's Web site. Obtaining a clear understanding of the corporate culture and the leadership style of senior management is essential to achieving career satisfaction. You can ask questions that elicit information on these subjects and help you to assess if this is the right environment for you.

If you want to know about the culture, you could ask:

1. Who is the most successful recent hire within your company, and what characteristics does that person possess that make him such a great contributor?

2. Tell me about some of the employees who have the longest tenure here, and what, in your opinion, has made them so loyal to the company?

3. Who in the organization would you say best personifies the culture of the company, and why?

4. How would you describe the company's management style and culture?

Notice these are all very positive questions designed to offer insight about who the powerful people in the organization are and why. It is great information to know so that you can observe them and learn from them if offered a position, helping you to achieve success by emulating them.

Do's and Don'ts
When Asking Questions

DO:

- Ask for a business card.

- Ask "How do you go about" questions.

- Ask what the next steps in the selection process are and if you can follow up.

- Ask if there is anything you can do to improve your candidacy.

- Ask positive, future-focused questions that incorporate you into the company.

DON'T:

- Ask yes/no questions.

- Ask negative questions.

- Ask about salary/benefits.

- Ask questions you know nothing about.

- Leave without asking any questions.

Attire

While most people understand the necessity of dressing well for an interview, there is confusion on how to dress when the company follows a business casual dress code. To clarify this confusion, always err on the side of conservatism. The company may be business casual, but you are not in the company, and until you are, apply the rules of interview attire and dress conservatively and formally.

The only exception is when a company representative specifically asks you to dress business casual. Dilbert says, "I love the business casual look for the way it combines unattractive with unprofessional while diminishing neither." Dressing business casual for interviews has been a challenge for 20 years, and people still struggle with it. While styles may change, the premise of business casual does not. The emphasis should remain on business, not casual. When business casual is requested for the interview, the simple, smart business casual wardrobe for men should include:

- Sport coat (solid navy or one with a subtle pattern)

- Dress pants (super wool for a more formal look, microfiber for more casual)

- Sport shirt

- Mock turtleneck or polo (three-button with collar) sweater

- Socks to match pants and shoes

- Brown or black belt

- Brown or black shoes (shoe and belt colors should be the same)

The simple, smart business casual wardrobe for women should include:

- Dressy matched trousers
- Black jacket with matching black skirt and trousers (sold as separates, but combine like a suit)
- Jacket with matching skirt and trousers in a versatile fabric and color
- Stylish white cotton shirt
- Lightweight knit sweater
- Low-heeled brown or black pumps
- Earrings, necklace, and belt to accessorize

Dressing conservative and formal is important. If you look successful and well-educated, people perceive you that way. Similarly, if you look unprofessional or casual, people will think you are unprofessional or lack serious interest in joining the company. In a perfect world, performance should represent 95 percent of business success; but the reality is that the split is 33 percent performance, 33 percent image, and 33 percent publicity. Here's some advice for dressing appropriately for the interview.

MEN:

- Buy the best suit you can afford.
- Buy the best shoes you can afford, and keep them in meticulous condition.
- Wear thin black dress socks (even with a navy or gray suit).
- Wear a white (no blue or ecru colors) 100 percent cotton long-sleeved shirt with $\frac{1}{4}$ inch to $\frac{1}{2}$ inch of cuff showing at the coat sleeve.
- Wear a crew-neck T-shirt, not a V-neck T-shirt, underneath.

- Do not wear cuff links.

- Make sure the shirt is professionally starched.

- Wear a 1-inch black leather belt with a simple rectangular belt buckle.

- Wear a 100 percent weight wool suit (except in summer). Second choice would be a 65 percent/35 percent poly blend.

- Wear a pin-striped, solid navy or charcoal gray suit.

- Wear a single-breasted suit coat.

- Wear a conservative tie with no pictures, paisley, or loud prints.

- Do not wear a tie bar or tie tack.

- Do not wear a handkerchief in the suit pocket.

- Do not wear heavy cologne; no cologne is preferred.

- Do not wear pinky rings, necklaces, or bracelets.

- Wear hair short (above the ears); no sideburns or facial hair preferred.

- Make sure hands are clean, nails are manicured, and cuticles groomed.

WOMEN:

- Buy the best shoes you can afford—navy or black closed-toe pumps with no decoration. Make sure there are no scuff marks, and don't wear heels higher than 2½ inches.

- Wear sheer or neutral hose.

- Wear a professionally dry-cleaned silk or cotton blouse with a high neckline.

- Wear a 100 percent weight wool suit (except in summer). Second choice would be a 65 percent/35 percent poly blend.

- Wear a solid dark-color suit with a single-breasted coat. If it is a skirt suit, the length should be long enough to cover the knees or at least four fingers from below the knee.

- Wear no more than one conservative ring on each hand.

- Wear only one bracelet, if at all.

- Wear one small silver, gold, or pearl necklace and small earrings that match.

- Wear a conservative hairstyle; no bows or clips in hair.

- Wear light makeup for day wear.

- Do not wear heavy perfume; no perfume is preferred.

- Make sure hands are clean, nails are manicured, and cuticles groomed.

Frequently Asked Interview Questions

It's important to remember that the information contained on your résumé will have a significant effect on the questions you are asked in an interview. Make sure you know your résumé, and prepare results-oriented stories to illustrate each of your accomplishments. Also, remember to prepare questions to ask the interviewer. Take the time to research the company, its products or services, the industry, and its competition. Here are likely questions you may be asked.

1. Tell me a little about yourself.
2. Why did you leave your last job (or why are considering leaving)?
3. Who is the worst (best) boss/subordinate/colleague you have ever worked with?

4. In your present position, what problems have you identified that were previously overlooked?

5. What kinds of people do you find it difficult to work with?

6. Describe a situation where your judgment proved to be valuable.

7. What aspects of your previous jobs have you disliked?

8. Do you work better under pressure or with time to plan and organize?

9. What is more important—completing a job on time or doing it right?

10. What are your strengths and weaknesses?

11. What are the three most important accomplishments in your career?

12. What kinds of decisions are most difficult for you?

13. What is it about your current company that you do not particularly like or agree with?

14. How would your boss describe you?

15. What three words would you choose to best describe yourself?

16. How do you go about criticizing others?

17. What type of tasks do you feel you cannot delegate?

18. Why do you consider this to be a good opportunity?

19. What kind of relationship and atmosphere do you prefer to maintain with colleagues and subordinates?

20. How do you try to develop the weaker members of your team?

21. Describe how you allocate your time and priorities on a typical day.

22. Could your team carry on without you? How?

23. How do you determine if a subordinate is doing a good job?

24. Are you a better planner or implementer?

25. Describe your impact on your present company.

You are now ready to articulate the value you bring employers. In the audition, you ready yourself for a wonderful future that is rewarding and satisfying. By influencing the hiring managers that your career goals are reflective of their needs, you set yourself up to take the stage and live a meaningful life rich with reward. The next two chapters are dedicated to the final important elements of your career search process. Here, you will learn to manage your career search process and conduct effective post-interview strategies. The devil can be in the details, and this portion makes sure that all bases have been covered and that you are completely ready for action. These action items include setting goals, conducting organizational profiles, completing productivity charts, creating references, writing high-impact thank-you letters, and learning how to negotiate the offer. This performance allows you to have what you have always wanted—a career that is not work but play . . . your play!

Lights, Camera, Action

THERE IS A MAGICAL point in any production when the play is performed and brought to life. It is where your audience comes in contact with your performance on opening night. This chapter is dedicated to bringing your career search to life through action plans and goal setting. It also describes ways to interact effectively during post-interview discussions.

Opportunities to launch the play of your life

> *"Make the beginning quick, the end quick, and put the two of them as close together as possible."*
>
> —George Burns

exist all around you. However, the opportunities do not become readily noticeable, even when they are right in front of you, until you actually own your internal career description.

Think about it this way. Do you remember buying your car? You probably started by observing cars on the road to see which ones you liked. Then you researched the cars to see which ones met your criteria. Next, you performed multiple test-drives in the ones most interesting to you. You mentally tried on each model for size, weighing the pros and cons of each one.

Once you made a decision, you bought the car, got the keys and title; this car was *yours*. Now you notice this car model more frequently than any others; in fact, you see your car model everywhere! This is not because the rest of the country went out and bought the same model. You have an increased awareness of this car because it is now connected with you.

It is natural for you to connect to and notice those things that are relevant to you. An important element of creating the play of your life is the ownership you feel for your script. Once you establish this ownership, you will begin to see opportunities to produce your own original play all around you.

Organize Your Network Strategy

Everything you come in contact with involves a profession, industry, or occupation, from the sweater you wear to the electricity in your home. Everything you see, taste, smell, hear, and feel is a result of someone's occupation. The sheer number of options can be overwhelming. Once you add to the challenge that those options are constantly evolving and changing, organizing your search becomes even more important.

You might assume that if there is so much opportunity, the best strategy is to keep options open and see what comes. In this scenario, information overloads you because of too much breadth and scope. With no reference point or strategy, the volume of opportunities shuts down your ability to engage the market in a meaningful way.

Having too many choices can make it nearly impossible to spend your time wisely. In order to make good choices, you need to be able to select among options, weighing the variables that impact those options and the pros and cons that come along with them.

Imagine you want a book. You go to the library and say to the librarian, "I want a book." The librarian will tell you there are millions of books, thousands of which are in this branch. The librarian will request that you look around until you find one that interests you. In this circumstance, you could be in that library for hours, days, weeks, or months before you actually settle on a book to read. The process is overwhelming, and because you do not know what you want, the librarian is unable to assist you.

If you know what kind of book you want, the librarian can help you. "I want a book about birds. I am interested particularly in learning about robins that live in Georgia." The librarian will direct you to the pertinent section in the library. The librarian may even recommend one or two that have received positive reviews from other bird-watching enthusiasts. In this scenario, you would receive a lot of assistance and would be out of the library in less than 5 minutes.

In order to network effectively, you must know the play of your life very well and be able to describe it without hesitation. You also must know what "production houses" (organizations) are most likely to produce it.

There are tangible and intangible factors to consider when generating a target list of organizations. Many of the intangible factors were assessed during the creation of the play of your life and include work environments and

FACTORS TO CONSIDER WHEN IDENTIFYING TARGET ORGANIZATIONS

- Use of degree skills
- Degree of responsibility
- Chance to develop new skills
- On-the-job training
- Variety of assignments
- Title
- Challenge
- Travel requirements
- Decision-making opportunities
- Career goals
- Personal growth potential
- Relevance of knowledge
- Relevance of experience
- Fulfilling long-range objectives
- Promotion potential
- Performance evaluation
- Opportunity for a mentor
- The organization
- Reputation
- Size
- Industry
- Management style
- Product/service offered
- Location
- Potential of organization
- Working conditions
- Corporate culture
- Personal goals
- Degree of sociability
- Rural or urban setting
- Career interests
- Time flexibility
- Personality needs
- Values and ethics
- Recreational habits
- Commute time
- Workplace variation
- Financial goals
- Salary
- Bonus
- Profit-sharing
- Stock options
- Insurance program
- Moving expenses
- Association memberships
- Educational assistance
- Vacation time
- Sick leave
- Health club

leadership styles. There are also important tangible factors to take into consideration. Review "Factors to Consider When Identifying Target Organizations" as you prepare to create your target list of organizations. After reviewing the factors, write down the 10 most important factors in your target organization profile.

Target Organization Profile

1.

2.

3.

4.

5.

6.

7.

8.

9.

10.

Now transfer the information above to the target organization analysis below. Provide the information as requested if it was not included in your 10 factors. The exercise below will help determine if your career search is feasible or if adjustments need to be made to ensure success in achieving your goals.

Target Organization Analysis

What is your target organization profile?

Location:

Industry:

Organization size:

Compensation:

Title:

Other factors from list above:

What is the annual availability of this profile?

If you are a physical therapist and your target organization is a large hospital in Phoenix, Arizona, then you want to identify how many large hospitals in Phoenix currently exist.

Total number of organizations that fit your criteria within the desired location: _____

Next, determine how many positions with your desired title are likely to be available in each of those companies. For example, there may be six physical therapist positions in each of the hospitals you target.

Total number of positions with your desired title within those organizations: _____

Total organizations multiplied by total positions equals total market opportunity: _____

In order to determine the total number of positions likely to become available within your target profile, you need to estimate the average length of time people stay in the same position. Remember that the average length of employment in today's fluid marketplace is 3 to 5 years.

Estimated annual turnover percentage in these organizations at this professional level: _____ Note that most mid-level and high-level executive positions turn over every 2 to 3 years. Keep in mind that employees retire, move, quit, get fired, die, and become disabled. New positions are also created as a result of organization growth.

Total market opportunity multiplied by annual turnover percentage equals your annual job availability: _____

What is your competitive advantage level?

Your competitive advantage level is a way to determine how your qualifications compare with those of others vying for a job and assess the likelihood of your getting that job. If your target profile is the same industry, same profession, same geographic location, same size, and same compensation range as your previous employer, your competitive advantage level is 80 percent—superior!

If your target profile is the same in at least three of the five criteria, with one or two being the same industry or profession, your competitive advantage level is 60 percent—very good.

If your target profile is the same in at least two of the five criteria, with one being the same industry or profession, your competitive advantage level is 40 percent—about average.

If your target profile is the same in at least one of the five criteria, your competitive advantage level is 20 percent—below average.

Your competitive advantage level: _____

What is your placement factor?

Annual job availability multiplied by competitive advantage level equals placement factor. For example, if there are 30 positions available annually and you have a very good (60 percent) competitive advantage, then it is likely that you will be considered for 18 opportunities in the course of a year.

What is your estimated length of search?

Estimated length of search is determined by how many opportunities are available to you over the course of a year. If there are a lot of opportunities, it will not take you as long to secure a position. A general estimation is shown on this chart.

Placement Factor	Months to Secure a Position
10 opportunities	12 months
20 opportunities	6 months
40 opportunities	3 months
80 opportunities	2 months
100 opportunities	1 month

Using the chart above, you can see that if there are 18 opportunities available, then it will take you approximately 7 months to achieve your career goal.

The analysis formulas above can help you determine a strategy that will best suit your needs. By experimenting with different criteria preferences, you can determine the estimated length of time each search process will entail.

Questions to ask yourself:

1. Is the search time reasonable?
2. Is the target market large enough?
3. Is the target market too large or too limited?
4. How can the target market be expanded to shorten search time if necessary?

Options for broadening your search:

- Expand geography
- Add market segments
- Expand positions
- Conduct dual campaigns
- Lower compensation requirements

Target analysis provides a framework for conducting your search strategically. By knowing exactly which companies you are targeting, you are in a better position to apply strategies that will help you introduce your qualifications to those organizations.

Remember that many new opportunities emerge every day, and the marketplace is becoming more fluid. While using Internet research tools and directories of companies and industries is helpful in creating your list, it is also important to look for opportunities to produce the play of your life in less obvious places.

Where can you go and what can you do to expand your target organization list?

_____

_____

_____

_____

_____

Target Organization List

List organizations that you would like to work for.

1. _____

2. _____

3. _____

4. _____

5. _____

6. _____

7. _____

8. _____

9. _____

10. _____

11. _____

12. _____

13. _____

14. _____

15. _____

Once you identify and list your target organizations and ensure that the list is realistic, the task of getting your qualifications in front of the hiring managers begins.

At this point, you need to inform your network of the specific organizations you are researching. The concept is not to get a job directly, but to get information and contacts related to your target organizations working for you.

Informational interviews serve a vital role in a strategic career search. These interviews are likely to provide opportunities that have not been advertised. Also, if you are referred by someone who is respected in the field or profession, you will obtain a competitive advantage.

Creating a Plan

Career searches can overwhelm even the most passionate people if they pursue opportunities haphazardly or without a plan. A plan that holds you accountable will help reduce the challenges posed by an increasingly nebulous marketplace. Structure is important because it allows you to put order and accountability into your career search. It is critical to monitor the results of your activities, actions, and efforts.

> *"Those who make the worst of their time most complain of its shortness."*
> —*Jean de La Bruyère*

Creating a productivity chart is useful for tracking the results of your efforts. Start by determining the amount of time that you are willing to commit to your career search. Next, break your activities into meaningful time allocations.

By tracking your activities, you can analyze how you spend your time and which strategies produce the best results. While time appears infinite, it is also the very element that seems to slip away quickly. If you spend a lot of time and do not see results, it is possible that your time is not being used wisely.

Productivity Chart

Keeping a productivity chart helps you monitor and manage your time. The productivity chart on page 227 breaks the search process into three areas: education/research, letters, and meetings. As you implement your career search, your productivity should transition from being heavily focused on education and research to being heavily focused on meetings and networking events.

EDUCATION

This first section involves completion of the exercises outlined in the previous chapters as well as earlier in this chapter. The specific research exercises you will complete during the career search education phase are:

- Network Generator (see page 179)
- Target Organization Profile (see page 219)
- Target Organization Analysis (see page 219)
- Target Organization List (see page 223)

Referring to the productivity chart on page 227, "Network by Phone" involves activity to generate meetings, and "Administration" involves follow-up letters, network letters, cover letters, and résumé enhancement/customization. These elements require a lot of time and energy early in your process but will trail off as you get further along in your search.

LETTERS

As your search progresses, you will send many letters to introduce your qualifications to employers and to penetrate the open market. In the "Letters" section of the chart, "Direct Mail" involves all letters you send that are not solicited by someone. "Ads" involves all letters sent to posted positions in the classifieds, job search engines, or organization Web sites. "Search Firms/Agencies" includes all letters sent to firms that have requested your qualifications for review.

MEETINGS

The vast majority of your activity occurs in "Meetings" as you move your search into full gear. "General Network" includes all meetings attended to expand your network, including meetings with search firms that do not have a specific position open. General networking includes meetings with anyone on your network list.

"Network Target Organization" focuses on meetings you attend to learn more about a specific organization. Target organization networking capitalizes on your ability to communicate clearly to your network the specific organizations to which you seek introduction. "Target Organization Peer" involves all meetings that engage a person within a target organization you have identified on your list. Generating these meetings is a direct result of your ability to integrate the six degrees of separation concept into your career search.

"Target Organization Hiring Manager" is self-explanatory and identifies your ability to create a compelling reason for someone internally to advocate on your behalf. And finally, "Target Organization Follow-Up" allows you to assess your effectiveness as you move forward in the selection process. This portion of the productivity chart provides insight into your interviewing capabilities.

PRODUCTIVITY CHART	
ACTIVITY	**TOTAL HOURS**

CAREER SEARCH EDUCATION
  Research
  Network by Phone
  Administration	

TOTAL CAREER SEARCH EDUCATION	

LETTERS
  Direct Mail
  Ads
  Search Firms/Agencies	

TOTAL LETTERS	

MEETINGS
  General Network
  Network Target Organization
  Target Organization Peer
  Target Organization Hiring Manager
  Target Organization Follow-Up	

TOTAL MEETINGS	

There is real power in the clarity and direction that emerge as a result of the exercises leading up to this point, but clearly defining a new career identity is not like facing a Biblical burning bush or stumbling into a hidden gold mine. *The Play of Your Life* enables you to identify work that is satisfying and rewarding, but even work that you love requires effort. There are typically no epiphanies or sudden reversals of fortune. The challenges inherent in making a change can lead to avoidance behaviors that sabotage your career search.

Avoidance Behavior

As you track the time spent on these activities, you can assess productivity barriers where you may unwittingly sabotage your efforts. One of the most common productivity barriers is avoidance behavior.

Networking is difficult because you put yourself in the market with the potential of being rejected. As a result, it is important to monitor if or when fear creates an obstacle to your success.

Avoidance behavior is the act of hiding behind your résumé, the Internet, or the phone to avoid rejection. When avoidance behavior affects your search, your rationale, whether you are conscious of it or not, is that you would rather receive no response to your résumé or e-mail than receive a negative response. If your career search strategy does not produce results, you could be sabotaging it with avoidance behavior.

Examples of avoidance behavior include:

- Spending more than 5 percent of your search time in Internet-related activities, such as posting your résumé on every search engine or surfing online search engines for opportunities and responding to them through e-mail

- Conducting direct-mail campaigns without follow-up, such as sending mass mailings to a broad list of companies (direct-mail campaigns constitute all unsolicited letters sent to prospective employers and recruiters)

- Responding only to advertisements in the newspaper

- Going to events where you already know all the people or to events where everyone else is there for the same career search purpose

You can learn a lot about your search by analyzing your productivity. If your career search has been under way for 2 months but you have not had a meeting with a hiring manager despite having sent out 100 responses to advertisements, perhaps you are engaging in avoidance behavior. If, on the other hand, you have had many interviews but have not obtained any offers, perhaps your interview skills need to be addressed.

Develop a good strategy and use tracking tools to assess how well your strategy is working. They ensure that you address the right problem at the right time. There was a piano player who was angry that his piano was always out of tune; he told the club owner that he would not play at his club again until the piano was fixed. When he returned to the club a month later, the piano was still out of tune. The piano player said to the owner, "I thought you fixed it." The club owner replied, "I did; I had it painted."

If you are not clear on what is not working in your career search, you may try to fix the wrong part. As a result, you could end up spending hours, days, even weeks, spinning your wheels. The more attention you pay to your activities, the more you will be able to assess what the real challenges are and how to address them.

Tracking activity is worthwhile only if you analyze the information and identify ways to improve your search. Much of what is called intelligence is simply the ability to recognize order in the form of patterns. Review your progress on a regular basis, analyzing results from the tracking tools for patterns.

What can you detect from your search to date?

Also, by tracking your activity in the productivity chart, you can assess how well your networking strategy is working. The objective of effective networking is to go deeper within a network, not broader. Talking to six people who are teachers is not as effective as talking to a member of the PTA who directs you to a teacher, who leads you to the principal, who directs you to the superintendent, who directs you to Human Resources, who then directs you to the human resources director of the neighboring school district who is in a position to hire someone with your skills.

As you plan your networking strategy, make sure your activities lead you closer to the end point and not to another surface contact. One recommendation to ensure your networking efforts stay on track is to keep a record, constantly reviewing your progress to determine that you are moving closer to your end point and who in your network has been tapped for information.

The process of networking can lead to burnout if not managed effectively. You can deter burnout by setting goals that ensure your stardom. STARS are goals you set for yourself that are:

S—Specific

T—Time-bound

A—Achievable

R—Realistic

S—Structured

The results of your networking efforts can be difficult to see; a direct cause-and-effect relationship is not completely in your control. When you feel like what happens in your life is not in your control, stress builds. In a study at Emory University several years ago, stress levels of race-car drivers were monitored as they sped along at high speeds. The drivers' stress levels were then monitored in the pit as the cars were serviced by the crews.

While it would seem more likely that the drivers' stress would be highest on the track, where one wrong move could kill them instantly, they were more stressed in the pit. The researchers concluded that in the pit is the only time the drivers are not in control. It was the only time they were relying on someone else to help them win the race.

The amount of control you possess has a direct connection to the amount of stress you experience in your career search. As a result, the implementation portion of your career search is one of the most difficult aspects of the entire process. When you begin networking, your search is no longer completely in your control. You must rely on the people and conditions around you to support your search efforts. In order to diminish the sense of being out of control, track your progress through goals that produce STARS.

Here are several examples of goals using the STARS technique.

- I will create and complete the first draft of my network list by 2 weeks from Monday.
- I will craft 10 networking questions that I want to use in building my network by 1 week from Tuesday.
- I will use the library to research associations and trade journals related to my profession/industry by 2 weeks from Wednesday.

Implementing a career search takes confidence, preparation, research, and action that is strategic and organized. With these activities in place, interviews will begin, and you will need to follow up effectively with thank-you letters, references, and negotiation tactics.

Thank-You Letters

Performing well in interviews is 90 percent of the battle. But if you want to solidify your chance for receiving the offer, send a thank-you letter within 24 hours.

Thank-you letters accomplish the following:

- Provide a great avenue to summarize your strengths and the benefit you bring to the organization.
- Address any skill area that you did not cover during the interview.
- Express your increased interest in the position as a result of your interview.

A thank-you letter should be one page. A handwritten thank-you is appropriate only if you are on a first-name basis with the interviewer. A formal letter is always preferred, however. Use first names only if you are on a first-name basis with the person. An e-mail thank-you is appropriate only if the hiring decision will be made within 24 hours from the interview and you cannot send a formal thank-you in time.

Content

The content of your thank-you letters should consist of four paragraphs.

PARAGRAPH ONE

Communicate your appreciation for the time and energy that organization personnel expended in the interview process. It is not necessary, but feel free to express how nice it was to meet the interviewer and the people who work there. Also, state that you are confident that you possess the necessary qualifications and that you are the best candidate for the position. Finally, express your increased interest in the position now that you have had the opportunity to learn more about the organization.

PARAGRAPH TWO

In your first sentence, note some important issue that the interviewer brought up that impressed you or that stands out about the position or organization. Your second sentence describes how you can add value or are in alignment with this point. The third sentence should offer an example illustrating this point.

PARAGRAPH THREE

Address any skill or quality you possess that you feel was not presented effectively in the interview. For example, if the interviewer asked about a certain technology that you did not know, take time here to address what you will do to become knowledgeable about this technology. Also, explain how you demonstrated an ability to learn new applications quickly in past positions. If possible, give an example of your ability to overcome this obstacle.

PARAGRAPH FOUR

Express your interest in receiving an offer and your willingness to furnish references who can speak to the very qualifications the hiring manager is seeking. Indicate that you will follow up within the week to learn about the next steps in the selection process.

Thank-You Letter Examples

On the following pages, you will find a couple of thank-you letter examples. Review them now and use them as a guide when you sit down to create your own letters.

THANK-YOU LETTER EXAMPLE

123 Smith Street, Anywhere, Florida 32807 • 321.244.4391

Date

Name
Title
Organization
Address

Dear Name:

Thank you for the opportunity on Monday, October 12, to discuss joining Eli Lilly. After meeting you and several members of the sales management team, my enthusiasm for your organization has grown even stronger. Your personal style and professionalism exemplify the characteristics that make Eli Lilly one of the world's leading pharmaceutical companies.

I was pleased to learn that your experience with Eli Lilly has brought you rewarding accomplishments and a high level of career satisfaction. Throughout my career with Abbott, I have had the good fortune to apply a high level of initiative, which has allowed me to excel in every position I've held. For example, while serving as a sales representative in Ross Medical-Nutritional Sales, I was the #1-ranked associate for outbound sales presentations and generated $3.5 million in annual revenues my first year. Additionally, I have successfully presented high-impact proposals to the executive staffs of 10 key accounts nationally that effectively persuaded favorable decisions. These accomplishments represent the quality and caliber of my experience and have brought me great career satisfaction.

After this initial interview, the leadership I witnessed has convinced me that your organization is the right match for me. I am also very confident that my extensive industry knowledge, sales and marketing strengths, and clinical experience in nursing offer the qualifications you seek.

Again, thank you for your time and consideration. I am excited to engage in the next step of the selection process.

Sincerely,

Interviewee Name

THANK-YOU LETTER EXAMPLE

345 Jones Street, New York, New York 10016 • 212-222-8900

Date

Name
Title
Organization
Address

Dear Name:

Thank you for the opportunity to discuss the director of finance position with the organization this afternoon. Since our interview, and in anticipation of a second meeting, I have given considerable thought to your questions, the expectations of the organization, and the challenges inherent in the assignment. To that end, I would like to bring several key points to the forefront.

• I offer progressive and accelerated advancement in management within the finance industry, having developed functional expertise that will easily transfer to the nonprofit community. My interests in joining your team are a desire to use my accounting talent in an organization that is aligned with my values and a commitment to creating healthy and supportive communities. I know the complexities of meeting budget constraints while maintaining the highest quality of customer service, and I am confident that I can provide the organization with tremendous benefit.

• While I have not had direct financial management experience in nonprofit, I am actively involved in CASA (Court Appointed Special Advocate) and the Westerville School system as a volunteer. My commitment to serving the community is a driving force in pursuing a career change, where I can contribute my professional expertise more effectively in the nonprofit arena.

• I am accustomed to leading, directing, and managing the day-to-day activities of a $4.5 million operation, a budget comparable to your agency's $5.5 million operating budget. Currently, I oversee 17 offices, where I lead the organization's financial development, manage a staff of nearly 400, and provide outstanding customer service to more than 30,000 clients annually.

On a more personal note, as my references will confirm, I am a dedicated, intelligent, and driven leader able to envision, motivate, and deliver results. Through these efforts, I have earned the respect of personnel from the front line staff to the organization's leadership.

I look forward to meeting you in the near future to discuss the next steps in the selection process. If you have any questions for me, please call me at 212-222-8900. Thank you.

Sincerely,

Interviewee Name

Follow-Up Strategies

The best time to communicate your value to a prospective employer is after the interview but before an offer. After the interview, you know more about the qualifications the interviewer is looking for in a top candidate. While thank-you letters are essential for showing your appreciation for the interviewer's time and energy, there are other ways to keep your candidacy vital. Thank-you letters are sufficient for highlighting the key points covered during the interview. Even better, though, is creating a customized post-interview proposal. This describes in more detail how you can contribute significantly to the employer. It is a very powerful strategy for differentiating yourself and clarifying how your experience specifically meets the organization's needs.

References

References are an important element of your marketing campaign. When a prospective employer asks for your references, it is a very good sign. References are not always checked by all employers. However, a reference check is mandatory when the applicant is responsible for money or caring for children, the disabled, or the elderly. It is important to identify who will serve as a reference in advance, and it is recommended that you have at least three references. Be aware that some employers will ask for as many as eight.

Selecting Your References

References can be current and past employers, colleagues, clients, customers, vendors, subordinates, personal friends, and high-profile individuals within your or their profession and/or industry. Select your references carefully. References need to reflect your status, quality, and professionalism. Also, remember that references are almost always contacted by telephone—with this in mind, whenever possible select references that will come across as positive and enthusiastic in a phone conversation.

Preparing Your References

When references are a part of the selection process, they become a valuable resource in helping you to outperform the competition. In order to help your references support your candidacy, make sure they have a current copy of your résumé and cover letter in addition to a copy of the position description. If possible, do not give your reference list to the hiring manager at the interview. Upon request, say you will furnish it within 24 hours, allowing yourself time to contact the references in advance of the hiring manager's call. This way you can prepare the references by explaining the interview process to date and advise them on what key areas of your strengths you want them to emphasize.

Your References as a Sales Tool

Upon submitting your reference list to the employer, explain your relationship to each reference and write a statement describing what core competencies this person can address. This strategy allows you to communicate your strengths in writing yet again, now emphasizing the specific areas discussed in the interview. Review the following example and create your own reference sheet.

FRAN C. SMITH

1153 Terry Avenue • Atlanta, Georgia 30306 • francsmith@aol.com • 404-555-1234

REFERENCES

Jane D. Green
Senior Vice President
The Crenshaw Organization
234 Glendale Avenue
Atlanta, Georgia 30305
404-123-5467 w

Jane Green served as my mentor and team leader during an expansion project to penetrate the European market. She can speak to my strengths as a team player and a project coordinator and my ability to complete multiple complex tasks on time and within tight budget constraints. She's observed and benefited from my analytical and strategic-planning skills and knows my ability to mobilize diverse groups operating both internally and externally toward a unified objective.

Sally Jones
President
Coca-Cola Foundation
1 Coca-Cola Plaza
Atlanta, Georgia 30311
404-258-3698

Sally Jones oversaw the key accounts I managed for her organization. She can speak to my relationship-building, customer service, and innovative thinking skills. Sally was a client of mine for over 6 years, and during that time frame I played an integral role in Coca-Cola's successful acquisition of three leading companies, making it the largest provider in the nation and third largest in the world.

Mark Brown
Project Manager
US Boxes, Inc.
123 Jones Street
Atlanta, Georgia 30360
404-857-9687

Mark Brown can speak to my expertise in leadership and performance management. Mark was one of my first hires as the manager of XYZ organization, where I was responsible for sourcing, recruiting, hiring, and developing a cross-functional team charged with launching a brand-new product line throughout the entire southeast division of the organization. Mark reported directly to me and received my guidance and resource support throughout the project. He knows how I manage teams, motivate people, and conduct performance evaluations.

Making the Deal

THE ART OF NEGOTIATING takes practice and skill, but it can be learned and performed by everyone. Upon receiving an offer, you need to be very clear on several important points before negotiating. Make sure you can say yes to the following statements:

> *"Desperation is the worst cologne."*
>
> —*Anonymous*

- I know and understand the specific requirements of the position.

- I know and understand where my position fits in the organizational chart.

- I know and understand how and when my performance will be evaluated.

- I know and understand the reporting relationships and have met all necessary people who will affect my success in this position.

If you do not have complete information on all of the statements above, obtain clarity on these items before engaging in a negotiation.

Preconceived Notions about Negotiating

Take a moment to ask yourself the questions below in order to assess your perception of the negotiation process. Identify any prejudices that can lead to self-sabotaging behaviors.

- Do you feel insulted for having to prove how much you are worth to an employer?

- Do you fear starting off on the wrong foot with your employer by engaging in the practice of negotiation?

- Do you feel pushy for asking for more than what is offered in the initial hiring proposal?

If you answered yes to any of these questions, it is likely that you could be your own worst enemy in the negotiation process. Employers typically expect to negotiate an offer. In fact, if you accept too quickly, they may speculate that they offered too much and wonder if you are really as valuable as they were led to believe.

Most people want to accept the offer, however, even if it is less than they hoped for, because they are completely drained by the process. I empathize with this and want to share an approach to negotiating that allows to you have your cake and eat it, too. If you know that you are going to accept the offer, do not attempt a hard-line negotiation with the prospective employer. This strategy could make them pull the offer. Instead, accept the offer, then negotiate it. It sounds strange, but it works fabulously. Once an employer decides that you are the right candidate and extends an offer, you, at that moment more than any other time, are more likely to get what you want. You are new and exciting, and the employer wants you to be happy. This is the time to discuss what your needs are and explore openly with them how to get those needs met. Here is an example.

EMPLOYER: We'd like to extend you an offer of $75,000 per year.

CANDIDATE: Thank you for selecting me as your top choice. I am excited to become a part of your team and assure you that you will be pleased with my performance. As you know, I am very interested in this position and feel very confident about joining your team, but I would like an opportunity to go over the details of the offer with my family, since my career impacts more than just me. When do you need a final decision?

EMPLOYER: We understand, certainly. How about by the end of the week?

CANDIDATE: Great. Again, this is a wonderful opportunity, and I look forward to reviewing the details of the compensation structure and benefits over the next few days and will get back to you as soon as possible, but no later than Friday afternoon. What is the best way to get a copy of the company's benefits and compensation plan, as it relates to the offer you just verbally extended?

EMPLOYER: Human Resources will prepare the letter and materials for you.

Later that week . . .

CANDIDATE: I had a fantastic conversation with my family and am ready to make a decision, but I have a few questions and am wondering what is a good time for me to meet with you in person.

EMPLOYER: This afternoon.

Later that afternoon . . .

CANDIDATE: First I want to express my appreciation for your time and assure you that you have the most qualified candidate for the position. And I want to be completely up-front in stating that I am 100 percent committed to you and am accepting your offer. Having said that, I do want to share with you several issues that came up during my analysis of the proposal and see if you have any flexibility or recommendations on how we can address several aspects of the offer I was hoping would be stronger.

EMPLOYER: Well, great, I am glad you are in—that is fantastic. Now, what are your needs?

CANDIDATE: Well, the compensation you offer in the letter is xx dollars. I was anticipating a starting salary closer to yy dollars. What can I do to get the compensation closer to this number? How flexible is this number?

Of course, you can ask any questions that are specific to your needs. The concept, though, is to accept the position, get on the same side of the table, and work as a team to help you get started on the best circumstances. By accepting and then discussing your needs, you position the conversation to take on a collegial tone, as opposed to my needs versus yours.

In this scenario, you are securing the offer so that it won't get pulled and at the same time letting the employer know that you would be happier if several minor changes were made to the compensation plan. If no changes can be made, then you will accept it as is. It is a good idea to discuss what you want early on because you have the most influence when you are new. The employer is excited to have you on board and wants to show the company's commitment to being a great place to work. Therefore, now is the time to ask open-ended questions. Examples of open-ended questions include:

- What would I need to do to be eligible for an extra week of vacation?

- How would I go about securing corporate funds to attend classes or professional development programs that enhance my performance?

- What is the policy on telecommuting? Is there one, and when has it ever been exercised?

- Describe for me the process for adding some new responsibilities as a means of increasing my compensation and advancing within the organization.

- How flexible is the company on flextime or other alternative working conditions?

By asking these questions or similar ones in an open-ended fashion, you position yourself to obtain clarity as opposed to expecting answers that meet your demands. Try to stay away from yes/no questions and questions that start with "Why." They close communication and put people on the defensive.

Negotiation Guidelines

Negotiating does not get relationships off to a bad start, but a poorly managed negotiation can cause unnecessary conflict. There is a protocol for negotiating that needs to be adhered to. Here are guidelines to follow.

- Do not accept the first offer immediately. Request that you be given time to consider the offer and discuss it with your family. Ask how much time they can permit.

- Do not expect them to give you a lot of time, but do not offer to get back to them in a day if they will give you 4 days. Let them define the time frame rather than imposing one on yourself.

- Do not negotiate over the phone if at all possible. It is difficult to judge the other party's response to your negotiating tactics over the phone. Being able to read and react to nonverbal language is very beneficial in negotiation. When you call to schedule a negotiation, say that you are pleased to have received the offer and reiterate your confidence in being able to make a significant impact on the organization. State that you have several items you would like to discuss in person.

- Do not position your negotiation strategy on past compensation if your salary history is not reflective of the new salary you are trying to obtain. Instead, position your negotiation to address the value of what you can do for the employer and the value you place on your abilities. If your past salary has been confined to standard incremental raises that are not reflective of your actual performance, discuss your salary requirements as they relate to your ability to outperform and exceed expectations. Request a slightly higher salary than the one offered (typically 10 to 15 percent higher) and offer justification for this adjustment.

- Do not negotiate more than once. If an employer meets your stated salary requirements, it is considered inappropriate to push for more. If the employer is unable to meet your stated salary requirements, inquire about possible adjustments that may be affordable in other areas of compensation. For example, if salary is nonnegotiable, can the company be flexible regarding vacation, continued training, benefits, or perks? Another way to reposition the negotiation if your salary requests are not met is to request increased responsibilities to justify a higher salary or ask for a performance review within 6 months instead of waiting a full year.

There are certainly exceptions to the above guidelines. Some employers do not negotiate offers at all. When this is the case, employers typically state this up front. They will also be forthright with the budgeted salary parameters. Some employers adhere to hiring procedures that prohibit negotiation, for equal employment reasons. When you receive an offer from one of these employers, it is considered inappropriate to engage in negotiation strategies. The good news is that these employers will almost always make their policies known up front.

Negotiation Tactics

Here is a brief description of some tactics that you can use when negotiating a deal.

Stalling

If you are waiting for another offer and want to stall the negotiating process, ask if you can schedule a day to shadow several key members. This will allow you to get a better feel for the culture and working environment. Request to speak to several clients or vendors to better assess the demands of the position. Request a copy of the organization's performance evaluation forms to better understand how you will be evaluated.

> *"Clothes make the man. Naked people have little or no influence in society."*
>
> —*Mark Twain*

There are times when it is appropriate to explain to the employer that you are committed to completing other employer interviews already scheduled. Request time to complete the selection process with these companies. If you make this request, tell the employer that you will not entertain any new opportunities or engage in future requests to interview with new companies.

Offer a specific date on which you will make a final decision. Most employers will understand that you want to accept the offer without ever having to second-guess or ask "what if."

Security and Assurances

It is a good idea in today's market to ask what you can expect if the position is changed or negatively affected through no fault of your performance. What assurances can the employer offer that you will be compensated should the organization have to downsize? Request a commitment to outplacement services and a minimum specified severance benefit that is in writing.

Determining Your Worth

Salary surveys are a great online resource and can also be found in print at the library. Jack Chapman's *Negotiating Your Salary: How to Make $1,000 a Minute* has a few other ways to determine this objective value, too. There is a shortcut for finding your salary range: call PinPoint Salary Service at 773-4-SALARY (773-472-5279). They will do research and give you a printout of your competitive range.

In summary, obtaining the career you really want requires you to apply powerful follow-up strategies, including thank-you letters, proposals, references, and negotiation. Post-interview activity can make the difference between auditioning and getting offered the part. Thank-you letters are standard protocol in the career search process. The ability to write a thank-you that not only expresses appreciation but also aligns your vision with the organization makes your letter stand out from the rest.

By integrating the concepts and principles outlined in this book, you can differentiate yourself and pull ahead of the competition. Adding a customized proposal to your post-interview process can further enhance your chances of getting the offer. Creating a reference page that highlights your skills and accomplishments most important to the organization is yet another effective way of communicating that you are, indeed, the best candidate. Finally, negotiating an offer that meets your expectations will allow you to perform the play of your life with greater satisfaction.

Review

The play of your life began with you because the best way to choose a career is to make sure you choose it. Although there are many theories of career development, there is no one method for identifying a career, just as there is no one way

> *"Life is not a dress rehearsal."*
>
> *—Anonymous*

to learn, live, and love. The decisions you make regarding your method of career development are influenced by a complex set of variables. Career decisions are impacted by your values, personality, talents, interests, and fascinations. While making a career choice is not about applying a simple formula, this book has given you information to make well-informed choices.

There is a reason behind everything you do or don't do; an internal logic to every choice you make or avoid making. In every moment, you act from choice, and the choices you make are formed by your passions. The process of self-discovery in this book is a pathway to understanding your passions and increasing your consciousness of what you are choosing. Knowing the truth about yourself is liberating; it offers you clarity and direction in a time when the environment cannot. The in-depth self-analysis you've completed may have been challenging, but it is this investment in understanding yourself that allows you to stop living as someone else's prop on the world's stage.

The Play of Your Life is about obtaining a career you love amidst globalization, innovation, and technology. Your script serves as the reference point for changing your career from work to play. Your ability to respond to change will be much stronger now that your level of self-awareness is heightened by the development of your script.

You are prepared to conduct a meaningful and strategic career search. You know how to explore this situation and can begin to identify and create exciting new opportunities for yourself that will lead you into a passionate career. You possess effective methods for implementing a search that produces results!

One final reminder: Be true to yourself. All the career advice in the world is useless if you are not being authentic. I know it can be difficult, especially when the realities of paying of the bills hit closer to home than you would like. But you must always keep in mind that you have valuable gifts to contribute in a meaningful way.

Remember that career development is a lifelong journey—something you continue to shape and create throughout your life. Your career satisfaction is not only about your job. As a society, most of us spend more time working than doing any other activity, so, more than likely, your professional happiness affects all other areas of your life.

My wish for you is to embrace every moment, even the tough ones. My goal is not merely to give you information or skills, but something more important—confidence in yourself and in your own ability to achieve happiness in your career.

When the going gets particularly tough, try not to lose perspective. Talk to other people who have persevered and achieved, and they will attest that the effort was worth it. Engage a career counselor to help serve as your production assistant. Advanced Career Development Incorporated has career counselors available to support you through each stage of the development process. We're located on the Web at www.ACDInet.com. Our virtual career center, also on the Web at www.playofyourlife.com, can get you in touch with a personal career counselor from any location with Internet access. For more information, call (877) 500-7039, or you can always e-mail me at csabatino@ACDInet.com.

You need not go at this alone.

This is the play of your life; make your performance meaningful.

Your stardom awaits.

INDEX